To Jane
Thanks for
Coming to our Womens
U.S. Open —

Perry Kurt Bell
2001

The Gift
Of Golf

MY LIFE WITH A WONDERFUL GAME

This book is dedicated to
my late husband and best friend, Bullet Bell.
Pine Needles was Bullet's dream and he built it
into a reality for me and our family.

Acknowledgements

This book is a joint effort of Pine Needles
Lodge and Golf Club and The Pilot.

Cover photograph courtesy of:
Michael Romney,
Legends Photographic

Photography in the center of the book courtesy of:
**Peggy Kirk Bell and
Pine Needles Lodge and Golf Club**

The Pilot
P.O. Box 58, Southern Pines, NC 28388

Pine Needles Lodge and Golf Club
P.O. Box 1915, Southern Pines, NC 28387

ISBN 0-9710917-0-6

Table of Contents

Foreword

Peggy Kirk Bell's love for the game of golf is exceeded only by the love for her family. She says golf has been wonderful to her. In truth, she has been wonderful for the game.

Golf has been life for Peggy Kirk Bell since her teenage years in Ohio. The game suited her competitive, yet self-effacing manner. In golf, she could always find a challenge — with her swing, the golf courses, and the other players. And when the round was over, she didn't have to extol her own virtues, the numbers on the scorecard did all the talking.

For Mrs. Bell, golf was never really just a game. It was a vehicle that carried her to places and heights that she could never have attained without it. Golf gave her friends, such as the late Babe Zaharias and the legendary Patty Berg. It played a role in her marriage to Warren "Bullet" Bell. It has provided a home at Pine Needles Resort, and given her a golfing family with daughters Bonnie and Peggy Ann and their husbands Pat McGowan and Kelly Miller. Her daughter-in-law, son Kirk's wife Holly, plays a vital role in the marketing of Pine Needles and Mid Pines.

Thus, it was Mrs. Bell's love for the game that eventually brought the U.S. Women's Open Championship to Pine Needles in 1996. The lives of too many USGA officials had been touched by this First Lady of Golf for her desires to be ignored.

And, once the USGA and the LPGA players had a taste of the wizardry of the Donald Ross-designed Pine Needles course, they could hardly wait until the final putt had been dropped by Annika Sorenstam to announce a return in 2001.

They couldn't wait that long to drop the bombshell that the 2007 Women's Open would be held at Pine Needles. USGA chairman of the Women's Committee broke the news at a gathering on Saturday night, while the formality of Karrie Webb's final round was still to be played.

It seemed somehow appropriate that the news of this announcement was broken to the golfing public by The Pilot, a small newspaper in Mrs. Bell's adopted town of Southern Pines that virtually scooped its competitive giants in a Sunday morning special edition.

The 2001 Women's Open was supposed to have been a showdown for LPGA Tour dominance between Webb and Sorenstam. Webb was the defending champion, while Sorenstam had won at Pine Needles in 1999 and was enjoying the best start of her professional career.

But Webb would have nothing to do with a so-called fight for supremacy. She took control with a Friday round of 65 and never looked back. While Sorenstam was struggling to shoot par, Webb was a perfectionist. Neither rain, nor heat, nor the pressures of defending her title could derail the Australian superstar.

"This means a tremendous amount to me," Webb said. "I feel fortunate to have won one U.S. Open, but to win two back to back, you can't put it into words. It's just a dream come true."

Webb used rounds of 70-65-69-69 for a 273 total that was one shot short of Sorenstam's record-setting score in 1999. It was strong enough to leave second-place Se Ri Pak of Korea eight shots off the pace. The difference proved to be Webb's ability to handle the intricacies of the Donald Ross greens. She used only 116 putts for the 72 holes, while Pak required 124.

The hospitality that Pine Needles and the Sandhills area provided for the USGA and the golfers obviously played a tremendous role in the decision to return in 2007. But the golf course itself was probably the most important factor.

Pine Needles course superintendent Dave Fruchte and his staff had the golf course in superb condition and, despite heavy rains on Friday that forced postponement of the second round, it held its own against the best women players in the world. Only Webb was able to break par.

"It's a great tribute," said Miller, chief operating officer of the resort, of the USGA's decision.

It was. To Pine Needles the golf course. And to Peggy Kirk Bell the matriarch.

Howard Ward
The Pilot Newspaper's Golf Writer

CHAPTER 1
What Golf Has Meant To Me

What do people do who don't play golf? I have no idea. I can't imagine not having golf as a centerpiece to my life.

I've always believed that God has a plan for all of us. We just have to be patient enough to let it unfold.

What if a friend of my father's hadn't moved to Texas and needed to sell that membership to Findlay Country Club back in 1939? Would I still have discovered golf?

What if my college roommate in Boston had not received that catalog to Rollins College in Florida, where it seemed to me the sun was always shining, the temperature always 70 or above, the emerald green of the fairways always beckoning?

What if I'd not run into the operators of the Mid Pines resort near Pinehurst that day in Florida in 1953? They suggested my fiancé, Bullet Bell, and I become partners with them in owning the Pine Needles course across the street, the one needing a new owner and some tender loving care.

What if that woman hadn't asked Bullet back in 1954 if someone could teach her to play golf, thus launching my career in golf instruction?

What if we had not, by pure luck, run into a man in 1957 who found us the capital to keep possession of Pine Needles and start building the hotel rooms we desperately needed?

It's humbling to think of the dominoes that fell one after another through my life that brought me in contact with this wonderful game. God was looking out for me, I can promise you that.

What a gift He's given me through the game of golf.

The places I've been. The friends I've made. The challenges I've faced. The competition I've enjoyed. The family that's grown up around golf. I can't imagine being any more blessed.

Growing up in Findlay, Ohio, I was a tomboy and loved all sports. At the age of twelve I decided I wanted to teach physical education and make a career out of sports. At the time, there were virtually no outlets for team competition for girls. I played the clarinet and trumpet in the high school band, and marching on the football field was as close as I got to organized athletics. Everything was intramurals, so teaching P.E. was the logical choice to further my involvement with athletics.

Until the age of seventeen, when my father purchased his friend's membership to the local country club, I knew nothing about golf.

It turned out that golf — not basketball or softball or even soccer, which was hardly played in this country sixty years ago — would be the perfect sport for me.

I found it more of a challenge than any sport I'd tried. You simply couldn't haul off and slam the

2

ball like you would a softball. It took dexterity, but you had to apply it properly. Power was nothing without timing in golf. I've always said, "It doesn't take a great athlete to be able to play golf. Conversely, great athletes aren't always good golfers." That's the beauty of the game.

The game of golf is filled with the very best people. Richard Tufts, the former owner of Pinehurst and a longtime administrator with the United States Golf Association, used to say that golf weeds bad people out because you're your own judge and jury on the golf course.

I might never have married Bullet if it weren't for golf. Our very first date was on the golf course. Golf was always a constant in our lives. It was the center of our business and it was our escape — we loved to sneak out for a friendly match.

Look at how my family has grown in golf. All three of our children — Bonnie, born in 1954, Peggy Ann (1958) and Kirk (1962) played golf as kids. They all played junior golf and college golf (Bonnie at the University of North Carolina, Peggy Ann and Kirk at the University of Alabama). Bonnie met her husband, Pat McGowan, a former Brigham Young University golfer and future PGA Tour player, when he stayed at Pine Needles while playing the Tour Qualifying School at Pinehurst in 1977. Peggy Ann met her husband, Kelly Miller, at Alabama, where they both played on the golf teams. Today I love watching my grandchildren learn to play the game. I have six (with twin boys due in July of

2001), and the three oldest are learning and enjoying the game. My youngest grandchild is the two-year-old daughter of Kirk and his wife, Holly, who played on the Yale University golf team. When she was born in 1999, I looked at those big hands and feet and said, "Gracie, you don't know it yet, but you're going to be a golfer!"

I've traveled the world with golf. I did a five-week exhibition tour of Australia in 1953 with Jackie Pung and the Bauer sisters and remember Alice Bauer addressing a shot as a snake slithered between her feet. I went to India for two weeks in 1994 to teach golf to a team of young women; cows wandered the streets and I stayed in a hotel with incense burning all over. I remember a trip to Great Britain in 1951 with the Weathervane Team, when I stayed in this English castle owned by Lord and Lady Brabazon of Tara. His car license plate read "FLYONE" for he was the first pilot in all of England and friend of the Wright brothers. The castle had no heat, so they took hot bricks, wrapped them up and put them in your bed for warmth. I remember thinking: How could I have visited this castle with hot bricks in my bed if not for golf? Even today at almost 80 years old I have great fun hosting European golf cruises for Kalos Tours.

And then there are all the great people I've met through golf.

One of my favorites was Bing Crosby, who lived along the fifteenth hole at Pebble Beach on the Monterey Peninsula of California. I lost in the second round of the 1948 U.S. Women's Amateur at Pebble Beach, and he came over and asked, "Would you like to play at Cypress Point with me tomorrow?"

I laughed and said, "I'm glad I lost."

Louise Suggs lost that day also, and she joined us. We had a great time. That was the beginning of a wonderful friendship. Bing visited Pinehurst in 1968 with baseball pitcher Gaylord Perry to hunt quail for *The American Sportsman* TV program. He came over to Pine Needles every night and sang with the little band that played nightly in our lounge. That week, he invited Bullet to play in his "Clam Bake" at Pebble Beach. That became one of the highlights of Bullet's year — traveling to the Crosby Clam Bake every winter. Bullet must have played in about seven of them before he had his first heart attack.

By pure coincidence, Bing was on the same ship I was on one year while traveling with my father to Scotland. I remember walking on deck every day, talking about golf with Bing. I could see the people watching us. They knew who Bing Crosby was, but I'm sure they were asking, "Who's the woman with Bing?"

I also met Bob Hope in the late 1940s at the National Celebrities Tournament in Washington, D.C. There was a dance the night before the tournament, and I was standing with a friend. I saw Bob and said, "There's Bob Hope!" My friend knew him and took me over to introduce me.

He said, "Bob, this is Peggy Kirk..."

Bob interrupted him and said, "Peggy Kirk from Findlay, Ohio!"

I was shocked! Bob Hope knew who I was! It turns out he was from Cleveland and, in fact, was part owner of the Cleveland Indians. He followed the golf news around the area and knew of me because I'd won the Ohio Women's State Championship three times.

Pete and Alice Dye have been great friends for at least fifty years. One year Bullet and I were visiting them at their home at Casa de Campo in the Dominican Republic. Their house sits right off the seventh hole, over the ocean, and I looked out one morning and saw this man making practice swings and digging big divots in their yard. I went out to him and said, "Hey, you can't do that. You're out-of-bounds. Do you know whose yard this is?"

He said, "Whose?"

"Pete Dye," I told him.

"Is he still alive?" the man asked. "I figured somebody would have *killed* him by now."

Obviously, he was having a bad day on the beautiful-but-perilous Teeth of the Dog course that Pete designed.

I can't begin to name all the other great friends in golf I've made. Arnold Palmer and Winnie always stayed at Pine Needles when the PGA Tour was playing Pinehurst No. 2 in the 1970s. Jack Nicklaus and I share Ohio roots, and being named to Jack's Captains' Club at Muirfield Village has been one of the greatest honors I've ever received. I look forward each May to going to The Memorial Tournament and seeing all the fellow members of the club — Peter Alliss, Judy Bell, Gary Player, Herbert Warren Wind, Bill Campbell and Bob Hope among them. Former President George H.W. Bush was recently named to the club, and it was an honor to meet him. It was a real tear-jerker at the 2000 Memorial when Jack was the tournament's honoree on its twenty-fifth anniversary. He almost broke up and so did the rest of us at the presentation ceremony when he talked about the influence and impact of four people in his life — his parents, Charlie and Helen Nicklaus; his golf teacher, Jack Grout; and his wife, Barbara.

Two of my favorite people in golf have been Arnold's and Jack's wives. Both Winnie and Barbara played big roles in the greatness each of their husbands achieved. I was heartbroken in 1999 when Winnie passed away.

I've played golf at Pine Needles with Supreme Court Justice Sandra Day O'Connor. She came to town in 2000 to speak to a group at Sandhills Community College. She and John Dempsey, the college president, came out to the course that afternoon and invited me to join them. Justice O'Connor is an avid golfer and a good one, too. In fact, she played better than I did that day.

Once in the 1950s, I played golf with Jackie Gleason. He was another serious golfer, and he had the first fancy golf cart I'd ever seen. It had everything on it — radio, ice chest, fancy wheels, a place for food and drink.

After Bullet died in 1984, my son-in-law Pat got a bunch of his friends from the PGA Tour to come to Pine Needles every November for a charity tournament we held in Bullet's honor. We called it the "Cheap Shot Invitational," and it ran for four years. We'd group one pro with three amateurs and add all kinds of crazy elements to the competition — like having three holes on one green, allowing mulligans on certain shots, requiring players to hit left-handed off the tee of the tenth hole, a shot requiring a hundred-yard carry over water. Paul Azinger in 1986 and Mike Donald in '88 each won the Cheap Shot the year before they won their first PGA Tour event, and we joked that winning it was a prerequisite to winning on tour. Once we decided to give away an "antique car" for a hole-in-one on the third hole. Craig Stadler made it and everyone thought we were talking about the A-Model that sits in front of the resort. Instead we had a beat-up, rusting truck with no doors or fenders as the prize sitting in the woods behind the green. At the end of the day, the pros gave a clinic on the range, and Craig slipped away. He surprised everyone when he came barrelling down the range in his newly won truck with a busted windshield and back-firing all the way! All the pros hopped on the back, and he took them for a spin.

In May of 2000, I met Tiger Woods at The Memorial outside the hotel where all the players were staying. I stood beside him to have my picture taken, and I told him I was surprised that he wasn't as big as I thought. "But I'm strong," he said. He's right about that. Tiger's shown there's a place for hard work in the gym as well as on the practice range in the game of golf.

And then there are all the great gals on the amateur golf circuit in the 1940s and the infant LPGA Tour in the 1950s. Many remain close friends today. Of course, one of the most special was Babe Didrikson Zaharias, the Olympic champion-turned-golfer who helped get the women's pro tour off the ground in the late-1940s. I probably should be paying Babe's estate royalties for all the stories I've told about her over the years. Sometimes we'll have a banquet at Pine Needles and my son-in-law Pat will come over and say, "Peg, you are the program tonight. Just tell a few Babe stories." That's one reason I decided—with some pushing from family and friends—to collect all these stories in this book. I wanted to get down on paper some of them before I forget them all.

Finally, what other sport beside golf would keep a seventy-nine-year-old churning with emotions like golf does with me today?

I was so frustrated with my game when I was at my winter home in Florida in early 2000. I was really struggling. I'd never played so badly. I was about to throw my clubs in the garbage. I said, "I'm just too old."

When I came back home in March, I complained to David Orr, our head instructor at Pine Needles Learning Center. He said, "Well, let's have a look at you." Before long he had me straightened out. I was breaking my left wrist down through impact. I wasn't extending *through* the ball. I went from hitting a six-iron on the par-three third hole at Pine Needles to an eight-iron. Now I can't wait to get back out there. In fact, we've incorporated the drills David had me doing into our golf schools at Pine Needles. I'm sure that David will one day be recognized as one of the great teachers of the game.

Isn't that something? I'm almost eighty years old and I'm still excited and striving to perfect my swing and play better golf.

Golf. It truly is a gift to those lucky enough to know it and love it.

Chapter 2

My Beginnings In Golf

I suppose it was quite appropriate that, coming from good Scottish stock, I would build my life around the Scottish game of golf. Despite those roots, however, golf was not part of my life growing up.

My paternal grandfather, David Kirk, was born in 1849 outside the village of Dunfermline near the east coast of central Scotland. He learned the milling business and decided at the age of twenty to come to America and make his fortune. He eventually settled in Akron, Ohio, the home of a major flour and corn mill manufacturer named Schumacher's (the company later became Quaker Oats). He found work there and saved his money. Soon he sent back to Scotland for his fiancée, Margaret Whyte. They were married in 1872 and had six children.

My grandfather was a big, strapping man and a diligent, hard worker. His boss at Schumacher's heard about a mill that had gone bankrupt in the town of Findlay, about two hours to the west, and recommended Grandfather Kirk to the bank as a good choice to take over the downtrodden operation from its creditors. So he moved his family to Findlay and eventually made a success of the mill. Later he renamed it Kirk Milling Company. I have on my kitchen wall some framed packaging from early Kirk Milling Co. products.

The church and the farm were the main influences on my mother's family. My maternal grandfather, Lester Boyce, was a Presbyterian minister. He lived with his wife, the former Grace Busby, in Findlay and later in Dayton, Ohio. There were three more ministers and two farmers on that side of the family.

My father, Robert Whyte Kirk, and my mother, Grace Boyce, met when my father was going to the Battle Creek Hospital in Michigan for treatment of his asthma and my mother was there with her mother, who had arthritis. As a child, my father was frail and doctors wondered if he'd live to adulthood. But he was tough and determined and, even though he weighed only a hundred and twenty pounds, liked to say he was "a lean horse for a long race." He lived to be ninety-four.

The union of my parents' families combined the values of discipline, hard work, thriftiness, an abiding belief in God and the workings of the church, and a respect for nature and the land. Education was important as well; my mother was one of the few college-educated women of the day because her father, as a Presbyterian minister, was paid no official salary but was provided the basic necessities by the church. That included a college education for his children. She received a degree in music from Wooster College in Ohio.

I spent a lot of my summers as a kid visiting my mother's family on their farms. Those were wonderful days. I remember the dinner bell, playing in the hay lofts in the barn, the Saturday night Grange meetings where the farmers would talk about pooling their money to buy new equipment. I think every child should spend some time on a farm. The lessons they learn are awe-inspiring. More than anything, farm people are deeply religious because they believe there's a higher power controlling the weather that affects their livelihood. There's nothing to make you realize your real stature in this world more than when droughts or floods affect your ability to provide for your family.

My twin siblings, David and Grace, were born in 1919, and I followed eighteen months later. I was born on October 28, 1921, and named Margaret Anne Kirk. I was always called Peg. Years later the golf press would start calling me "Peggy," but to this day around Findlay I'm still known as Peg.

My father was sharp at business, and we were blessed financially. He was in the wholesale grocery business, which survived pretty well during the Depression. "People have to eat, so we're in the right business," he'd say. He also had a sporting goods store, some interest in one of the early car dealerships in Findlay, and he made some pretty smart land deals. He bought an old school building one year, and everyone in town told him he was crazy. But he had the school demolished, and with the bricks he built on the same site an automobile repair garage, a body-works shop, a gas station and a dry cleaners. He had enough brick left over to build three small houses on lots he owned around town. He used those as rental property.

My father's businesses provided work opportunities for me and my brother and sister. One summer my job was to apply state tax stamps to cigarette packs. My dad told me, "You're the boss's daughter, so you have to work harder. No goofing off." I got paid ten cents an hour, and two other women got twenty cents an hour.

I told him, "That's not fair. They're making double what I'm getting and I work faster than they do."

He told me, "They have to pay rent and bills and support children. You don't have any obligations like they do. You get ten cents." So that was the end of that.

Since I was twelve years old, I wanted to be a physical education teacher. I was a tomboy growing up, and I played every sport I could. My parents remember me playing with a baseball mitt instead of dolls. I played a lot with the boys — skating, bowling, ice hockey, you name it — and tagged along with my brother. I was pretty athletic, and sports came naturally to me. I loved watching sports, too. We were 100 miles from Cleveland, and I remember some neighborhood kids getting together, hopping on the train and riding into Cleveland to see the Indians play baseball. We could leave in the morning, see the game, eat hot dogs, ride home, and spend about three dollars. I have the best memories of watching those old baseball players, guys like Bob Feller and Hank Greenberg. I was so impressed with them. Baseball was the top sport back then. We'd sit on the porch on summer afternoons and listen to the games on the radio.

There were hardly any girls' teams in organized sports in the 1930s, so most all of our competition

14

was in intramurals. My favorite class was gym class. So I thought being a P.E. teacher would be a perfect way to make a living.

Findlay was a nice little town of some twenty thousand people about an hour south of Toledo and Lake Érie. Headquarters for Marathon Oil and Cooper Tire were the major influences on the community. There must have been fifty kids growing up within a three-block range of our house on Hurd Avenue, so there was always plenty of activity around our house. Every game you can imagine, we played.

I was fascinated with cars growing up and at age sixteen, I bought a 1928 Oakland Roadster for $57.50 — the sum total of my working all summer in the warehouse. My father probably spent three times that amount putting new tires, a top and a muffler on the car. About four years later, after my second year of college, he bought me a new Packard convertible. He donated my old car to the war effort; they melted scrap metal down to make bullets. He told me, "There's a war on. They're not going to be making many cars for a few years. You need a good one."

Today I own nine cars, if you can believe that, including two 1928 Ford A-Models. The one that sometimes sits in front at Pine Needles was orginally sold to us by Wiffi Smith and was driven all over the country on the golf tour. She sold it to us around 1955. I've always been a Ford woman — I've got a 1978 Lincoln Mark 5, a 1987 Lincoln Limosine and a 1997 Lincoln Mark 8. I've also got a 1972 Austin London Taxie and a 1989 Cadillac convertible. However, my favorite cars are my convertibles a 1964 Lincoln and a 1966 Ford Mustang.

It wasn't until the summer of 1939 that the game of golf entered my life. Most every summer growing up, I'd gone to camp in New Hampshire, and I really looked forward to all the swimming and hiking and canoeing we did. But that summer my mother said I was too old to go to camp, that it was time to begin getting ready for college in the fall.

"What am I supposed to do all summer?" I asked, dreading a summer without camp.

"I don't know, but you are staying home," my mother said.

My dad had an announcement one night at dinner. A friend of his had recently moved to Texas and needed to sell his membership at Findlay Country Club. So dad bought it.

"You can learn to play golf if you'd like," he said.

"Golf?" I said.

I didn't know anything about the game, but I figured what the heck, it's something to do. My dad had a sporting goods store as part of his wholesale grocery business, and I went there and picked up some clubs — a three-wood, three, five, seven and nine-irons and a putter, and three golf balls. Back then, they didn't have wedges. You just laid your nine-iron open if you wanted to hit it higher or blast out of the sand. I played with that first set of clubs for two years.

I knew nothing about using those clubs, but undaunted, I went to Findlay Country Club, where a man named Leonard Schmutte was the professional. I went to the first tee, still having no idea what I was doing. I gripped the three-wood like a baseball bat and hit every ball into the woods. I lost all three and never made it to the first green. I went back into the clubhouse, found the "Professor," as I called him, and asked him how to hold the club. He looked at my strong grip and my baseball motion and asked if I'd like a golf lesson.

"Yes," I answered. "Can we go right now?"

"I'm afraid not," he said. "I have to mind the shop. But you be here at nine o'clock in the morning."

So over that summer of 1939, the golf bug bit me. And bit hard.

Leonard had traveled the pro tour with Horton Smith in his younger years before getting married and settling into the life of a club professional, and he had become an excellent teacher. He taught me grip, stance, alignment, swing plane, follow through, footwork, chipping, pitching, putting, sand play and course management. Lessons cost about a dollar, but he never charged me a dime. I'd get to the club early in the morning, before the pro shop opened, and chip and putt. When they opened, I'd get balls and hit them all morning. Then in the afternoon, I'd go out and play. He insisted that I spend the same time on my short game as I did on my full swing.

I couldn't get enough of this fascinating game. I was fortunate in having a good bit of athletic ability, but that alone wasn't enough. I hit those balls literally every direction imaginable. That was one thing that challenged me so much. Power without timing and precision wasn't anything. We'd be on the practice tee, and I'd swing and slice or hook the ball and Leonard would say, "Good swing." I didn't care how my swing looked; I wanted to hit it long and straight.

I'm not sure I ever broke a hundred that first summer, but I had fun trying. And I set some pretty lofty goals early on. I read about the Curtis Cup Match, the biennial team competition between lady amateurs in the United States against Great Britain and Ireland. It had the look and feel of the Olympics to me, and I was a big fan of the Olympics and Olympic athletes. Playing for your country was an impressive notion. So I decided I wanted to be on a Curtis Cup team. Playing golf for the glory of the Stars and Stripes — that seemed to me to be the ultimate.

My first summer of golf was short lived. In September I was off to Sargent's Physical Education School in Boston (now a part of Boston University) to study for a career in teaching. I took my golf clubs with me but never got to play. I didn't have a car (in those days you couldn't have a car at college until the last semester of your senior year), so it was difficult to get out to a golf course, and besides, I didn't have any time. And the weather in Boston during the school year isn't very conducive to developing your golf game.

So I went back home to Findlay for two months the following summer and reacquainted myself with the game. I made more improvement that summer, and in fact, won the women's club championship. That's not saying a lot, though, because the competition wasn't very strong. Ninety was a great score. I probably shot somewhere in the eighties and won the championship. I wasn't sure what the future held, but Leonard saw some potential. "She gives promise of being the best woman golfer I have ever known, and I have known quite a few," he told the local newspaper.

During spring break my second year at Sargent, I visited my parents, who were spending the winter in North Miami. It was snowing when I left Boston, but I got to Florida and it was warm and sunny. I said to myself, "I've got to find a way to get to Florida." I was excited about the idea of playing golf year-round there.

When I returned to Boston, I found a stack of college catalogs my roommate had gathered. One was from Rollins College, a small, private institution located just outside Orlando. It had all these beautiful pictures of the Florida lifestyle and kids with smiles on their faces. I said, "This place is for me." So I transferred to Rollins to begin the 1941 school year.

There was no women's golf team at Rollins, but every one of the twelve hundred students there was a member of Dubsdread Country Club. That didn't mean anything to most of them. They just wanted to use the swimming pool. But about twenty of us played golf. All my classes were in the morning, so by noon every day I was on the golf course. It was a great life. I also joined Kappa Kappa Gamma sorority, and I can't tell you how many women I've met over the years in golf that are Kappas. My daughters, Bonnie and Peggy Ann, are also Kappas and also have degrees in physical education — just like their old lady!

I was delighted during my college days to get an upgrade on the old set of Wilson clubs I'd gotten from my dad's store. My uncle, Harry Spitler, was a good golfer in Cleveland. He was visiting us and told my dad those clubs were no good for an avid young golfer. "Bob, get this girl some real clubs," he said. So my dad bought me a set of custom-made clubs from Kenneth Smith, who for many years was the leader in the custom-club business. I had that same set for years until I turned pro.

During this period, I got my first exposure to tournament golf. A lot of the men professionals hung out at Dubsdread during the winter, and they had an alternate-shot tournament with the pros and locals called the Florida Mixed Two-Ball. I teamed to win one year with Joe Kirkwood Sr., the famous and only trick-shot artist of the day. He thought I was the perfect partner for him — Kirkwood & Kirk.

One day I noticed a little item in the newspaper about the Women's North and South Amateur in a place called Pinehurst.

"Pinehurst," I said. "That's the golf capital of the world. Gosh, I need to go play in that tournament."

So I bundled up some clothes, tossed my golf clubs into my Packard convertible and set off for Pinehurst. When I got there, I went to the registration desk in the clubhouse and said, "I'd like to enter the North and South. What is the entry fee?"

The tournament official wrinkled his brow.

"There is no entry fee," he said. "This is an *invitational* tournament."

I wanted to crawl under a rug. I felt horrible. I was just a dumb college kid showing up unannounced at this famous golf resort.

"Wait here and I'll be right back," the man said.

A few minutes later, a distinguished looking man with wire-rimmed glasses presented himself.

"Hello," he said. "I'm Richard Tufts, and I'd like to extend an invitation to you to play in the North and South."

It was my first trip to Pinehurst, and I *crashed* the party. I was unbelievably green. Mr. Tufts was so gracious to handle it that way. He and I would go on to be good friends. He was delighted when Bullet and I bought Pine Needles in 1953, and later the Bank of Pinehurst, which the Tufts controlled, loaned us money for some expansion we needed to make.

Among the friends I made playing in the North and South was a girl named Buttons Cosgrove (who later married Julius Boros). At the time, Buttons' parents were employees at Pinehurst Country Club but soon would move a few miles down Midland Road to Southern Pines to take over management of Mid Pines Country Club. Our friendship flourished, and over the next few years, as I graduated from college and began playing the women's amateur circuit regularly, I'd visit Mid Pines every year between Thanksgiving and Christmas to work on my golf game.

Little did I know how important the Cosgroves, Mid Pines and the Pinehurst area would be in my life.

But for now, all I wanted to do was play golf. When I graduated from Rollins in 1943, that's what I set out to do.

CHAPTER 3
My Life On The Amateur Tour

You can talk all you want about the money in golf today, about the club-making technology, about the agronomy that makes golf courses so velvety smooth. You can talk about the coast-to-coast travel, all the media coverage and the golf academies.

As good as we might have things today in golf with our modern bells and whistles, I want to tell you: There is nothing that could beat life on the old amateur golf tour. I get emotional just thinking about the life we led, the fun we had, the innocence of that long-ago era.

I never gave a moment's thought to being a golf professional. There was no money in the game back in the 1940s, there were hardly any women pros, and the position of a golf pro long ago wasn't held in as high a regard as it is today. For a long time, pros weren't even allowed in the clubhouse of some country clubs. Amateur golf was the thing. Some of the best players never turned pro. Bobby Jones was the perfect example. He led an exemplary life by practicing law in Atlanta and playing golf during the spring and summer. Bill Campbell is another great amateur. He's been in the insurance business in Huntington, West Virginia, all his adult life, playing amateur golf and giving back to the game through his work on various committees within the

USGA. He was also captain of the Royal & Ancient Golf Club of St. Andrews, Scotland. Harvie Ward, who now teaches at Pine Needles, had a great amateur career in the late 1940s and early 1950s but didn't turn pro at the time because the money wasn't attractive, and he felt he would enjoy his golf life more as an amateur.

We played simply because we loved the game, we loved the competition, we loved the camaraderie of the amateur circuit. The only prizes were a silver cup and our picture in the paper. Money, agents, contracts and sponsorships never were a part of it. People went to college, graduated, got a job or began raising a family and played amateur golf tournaments whenever they could. That's really all I ever wanted to do. We didn't know that one day someone like Tiger Woods would turn pro three years into college and instantly become a millionaire many times over. I assume we'd have done the same thing if given that opportunity, but for us, playing the game was enough reward.

I remember when JoAnne Carner was inducted into the PGA World Golf Hall of Fame. She said, "The happiest days of my life were my amateur days." What a statement for a professional to make!

When I graduated from Rollins College in 1943, I decided I didn't want to teach school. I had an unpleasant student-teaching experience at a junior high in Orlando my last year at Rollins, and with World War II in high gear, my father needed my help in the family business at home in Findlay. So I returned home and made sales calls on the grocery stores, helped in the war effort, and played tournament golf whenever I could.

The next seven years would be my golden era in golf. My father did not believe in women working, so he was happy to support my amateur golf. When I turned twenty-five, he gave me some rental property, and I got to keep the income in return for managing the property. That first year, 1946, I spent every dime traveling the country and going to England to play golf. He never said a word about having to pay taxes on that income. You can imagine the shock when the tax bill came due in April.

Dad said, "Where is the tax you have to pay by April 15th?"

I said, "What tax?" I didn't know anything about taxes.

He wanted to see how I managed my money, and I obviously failed his test. I felt awful.

At that point I said, "I'm going to make my own money." I learned a good lesson from that experience.

One of the first big tournaments I played in came in 1941 when I was at Sargent College. It was the inaugural Women's National Intercollegiate, which was held at Ohio State University in Columbus. I won consolation honors in the second flight. That's where I first saw and met Patty Berg. She was one of the handful of lady professionals and was on Wilson's staff. Her job was to travel the country, give exhibitions and clinics, and promote Wilson clubs. She had a salesman travel with her. Her ability with a golf club was something to behold. She could hook the ball and slice it and hit it high and low — all on command.

"Amazing," I said. "She knows where it's going!"

My friendship with Babe Zaharias began at the 1945 Women's Western Open. Babe's mother had just died, and I expected her to withdraw. But she didn't. "I'm going to win this for my mother," she said — and of course did.

There was a loosely organized tour of women's events that included at least nine amateur tournaments in Florida: Miami, Hollywood, Palm Beach, Everglades, Daytona, St. Augustine, Ormond Beach, Orlando and St. Petersburg. My mother died in 1946, and my father bought a house in Hollywood, Florida, which he used on occasion and which provided a home base for me during the winters to play the Florida tour.

Then the tour moved north, going in April to Augusta for the Titleholders and Pinehurst for the North and South Amateur. There was the Eastern Amateur and the National Amateur, which was always my No. 1 goal. We had the Western Amateur and Western Open, the Women's Texas Open, the All-American and World Championship at Tam O'Shanter in Chicago.

I'd won two events partnered with other players — the Florida Mixed Two-Ball with Joe Kirkwood and the Women's International Four-Ball with Babe — but the Ohio Women's Golf Championship in 1947 was my first big win on my own. I qualified with a 69. It was the first time I had ever broken 70. I beat Jean Hopkins of Cleveland two-and-one in thirty-six holes at Akron Portage Country Club. That was an important win for me. The Babe said, "Peg once ya win one it gets easy."

I always felt like I was a good player, but it would be a stretch to say I was a great player. Most tournaments were match play, with two rounds of qualifying at the beginning. I won a bunch of medalist honors, but more often than I'd like I'd slip during match play. For some reason, I just didn't have the confidence you needed to stand above the masses. I remember talking to Louise Suggs once about how good Babe was. I'd just lost to Babe in the Western at Des Moines, and I said, "Okay, Louise, you get her tomorrow," as if it were a given that Babe would win.

Louise said, "I can beat her." And she did. That's the way Louise thought. But I never thought I could beat Babe. I guess I got beaten down mentally playing most every practice round and many exhibitions with her and watching her out-drive everyone.

Probably the best tournament I ever played was the Titleholders Championship in 1949 which I won. This tournament was held in Augusta each spring and was certainly a "major." The tournament was the brainchild of an Augusta golfer named Dorothy Manice, who envisioned an invitational comprised of "titled champions" of the top professional and amateur tournaments around the country as well as selected players from France, England, Scotland and Canada. The concept was "a Masters for the women." Patty Berg won the first three in 1937, '38 and '39, and the event was off and running. It was played just before the Masters at Augusta Country Club, just a stone's throw from Augusta National Golf Club.

During this era, making the Curtis Cup team was the ultimate goal for every woman golfer on both sides of the Atlantic. The Curtis Cup Match was the result of more than two decades of effort on the part of Boston sisters, Margaret and Harriot

Curtis. They'd traveled to England in 1905 for the British Ladies Championship and, along with several other Americans, played an informal competition against locals. Logistics, finances, politics and lack of widespread interest prohibited their idea from germinating until 1932, when the Ladies Golf Union of Great Britain and the United States Golf Association agreed to hold the Curtis Cup Match every other year.

I'll never forget a dinner held for the 1948 Curtis Cup team in New York before we left for England. Margaret Curtis got up to speak and told us what a great honor it was for us, that the Curtis Cup Match was a wonderful thing, and she hoped we'd *lose*. I was shocked. Here was the American founder of this event telling the American team she hoped we'd lose. I couldn't believe it. What I didn't understand at the time was the real meaning behind the competition. Great Britain had just finished fighting the war in its own backyard and there was virtually no golf played there during the war. Besides, the British team had never won the Curtis Cup. Margaret thought it best for the future of the match that the competition even out a little. That was a message that I later understood when I began to make good friends with the British players. That didn't make me want to win any less, but it helped me keep the competition in perspective.

Because of World War II, the Curtis Cup was suspended from 1940-46, but when it resumed in 1947, making the team was my primary goal. Unfortunately, I lost to Polly Riley at Pebble Beach in an early round of the Women's Amateur. Your standing at the Amateur was a key qualifying point for the team, and I just missed making the six-woman team. I was, however, second alternate. I made the trip to England with the team to watch the Cup matches held at Birkdale Golf Club and to compete in the British Amateur. The United States won the competition, 6½ to 2½. After the matches, several of us, including my golfing friends Buttons and Jean Cosgrove, were driven to St. Andrews in a Rolls-Royce limosine arranged by the father of my friend, Marjorie Row. Her dad was the president of Chrysler Motors in Canada. We teed off on the Old Course at 10 p.m. and within an hour word had spread around town that a group of top American amateurs was playing. By the sixth or seventh hole, we had a gallery of several hundred people following us. What a great thrill it was for us to play St. Andrews — the birth place of golf.

Finally, in 1950, I made the team handily after winning the Titleholders, North and South Amateur and Eastern Amateur. I joined Polly Riley, Beverly Hanson, Dorothy Kirby, Dorothy Kielty, Grace Lencyzk, Dorothy Germain Porter and Helen Sigel on the team that would face Great Britain and Ireland at the Country Club of Buffalo in Williamsville, N.Y.

Our captain was Glenna Collett Vare. Glenna was enjoying the twilight of an outstanding career that included six wins in the U.S. Women's Amateur from 1922-35. Though she was past her competitive prime when I came along, I admired Glenna for her ability and what she'd meant to women's golf. She managed a golf career and a family. She was also very shy and modest. She was

28

always saying how Joyce Wethered was the best player and how JoAnne Carner would have won more amateur championships than she if JoAnne hadn't turned pro.

What's interesting is that, although the thought of owning Pine Needles had never crossed my mind in 1950, Glenna had spent a lot of time during the winters at Pine Needles in the late-1930s and had sold a number of the residential lots around the golf course. Glenna worked for George Dunlap Jr., the U.S. Amateur champion who owned Pine Needles at the time. I look back and think — she's my idol and she once was involved in the golf course I now own!

Glenna was also renowned for a certain other ability — that of finding four-leaf clovers. Everyone knew she had this special gift. Maybe that's why she was such a great putter — she could see the lines and slopes so clearly.

We had a two-to-one lead after the first day's foursomes competition, but I was distraught at having lost, along with Helen Sigel, my closest friend, in our alternate-shot match. I'd finally realized my dream of playing for my country, but it turned out the pressure was more than I could stand. That night, I was petrified at the thought of playing singles the next day. I went and knocked on Glenna's door. I said, "Please don't play me."

But Glenna was tough. She said, "I'm the captain, and you're playing."

I was on the sixteenth fairway the next day in my match against Jeanne Bisgood when Glenna approached.

"How do you stand?" she asked.

"I'm one-down," I told her.

Glenna walked off and then returned in a couple of minutes. She handed me a four-leaf clover and said, "Go get her."

I won seventeen to tie the match. We both reached the eighteenth green in two shots and then Jeanne encountered one of the toughest shots in golf at that time — a stymie. Anyone under fifty doesn't know what a stymie is. The rule at the time was that only a ball six inches from the cup or one within six inches of your opponent's ball on the green could be marked and lifted. Scorecards were exactly six inches long and were used as measuring devices. If your opponent's ball was outside six inches, it stayed where it was when you played, meaning you had to go over or around it. You practiced for such situations, hitting little nine-iron chip shots over a ball that rested between your ball and the cup.

That day I putted first, to about seven inches from the cup. Jeanne's putt stopped about two feet short of mine, right on line with my ball. She had stymied herself. She had to practically chip it over my ball and straight into the cup. It was almost an impossible shot. She missed and I won the match, one-up.

And I still have that four-leaf clover that Glenna gave me on the sixteenth hole.

Those memories of the Curtis Cup give me goose bumps today. Almost every other year since then, I've attended the match and relived old times with the former British players. We have a competition among former Curtis Cup players called the Saucer, and each time Jeanne Bisgood (now a retired lawyer) and I replay our match from 1950. One of my best British friends is Mureen Garrett, who visits me at Pine Needles and has sent her grandson to our Youth Camp. The Curtis Cup was my first goal in golf and lives today as one of my fondest memories.

I could have been content to continue playing amateur golf for the rest of my life. But by this time, Babe and Patty had just gotten the LPGA Tour off the ground and kept tugging me to come join the professional ranks. Then Spalding came along and offered me $8,000 a year to play their clubs and use my name on clubs sold by Sears. I also was to give exhibitions between tournaments. I finally said okay, and I turned pro on November 1, 1950, after the Curtis Cup. I played my first professional tournament in early 1951 at the Ponte Vedra Inn, outside Jacksonville, Fla., and another chapter in my life with a great game unfolded.

CHAPTER 4
My Days As A Pro

Herbert Warren Wind, the great golf writer, is a good friend and has been a frequent visitor to Pine Needles over the years. One time I got a kick out of an article he wrote in *Sports Illustrated* about the beginnings of women's golf. He said that Mrs. Charles Brown shot a sixty-nine and a sixty-three to win our first Women's National Amateur.

Then came his kicker: "These happened to be her scores for the front and back nines, of course...."

I guess a score of 132 for eighteen holes back in 1895 was good enough to win. Fifty years later, though, our game had come a long way, and it was time to begin turning it into the big business that women's golf is today.

As my golf game developed over the 1940s, I never had any interest in becoming a professional. But as Babe Zaharias, Patty Berg and the other pros started to get things rolling on the new Ladies Professional Golf Association Tour in 1950, I began to have second thoughts. Spalding offered me $8,000 a year, decent money in those days, to play their clubs, plus royalties on the sale of Peggy Kirk Clubs and expenses to exhibitions and clincis. I finally said, "Why not?" Had I taken a job as a physical education teacher, I would be making $2,000 a year, and all I wanted to do was play golf.

I wasn't married (Bullet and I didn't tie the knot until 1953).

There was only a handful of women professionals in the early 1940s, and the only impetus for becoming a pro was to give lessons, work in a pro shop or represent an equipment manufacturer. It certainly wasn't for the money available in tournaments. In fact, until 1946 there were only three tournaments open to women pros: the Women's Western Open, the Titleholders, and the Texas Women's Open. The Women's National Open was inaugurated in 1946, opening one more opportunity for professionals. All of this began changing in 1947 when Babe turned professional.

Helen Hicks was the first woman professional of any national note, turning pro in 1935 at the age of twenty-three and signing with the Wilson Sporting Goods Company, an innovator in the belief that sports stars could sell products. Opal Hill, who played on three Curtis Cup teams in the 1930s, turned pro late in the decade after the death of her husband. Helen Dettweiler was another Wilson representative and early pro. Patty burst onto the national scene in 1935 by finishing second to Glenna Collett Vare in the National Amateur. She won the 1938 Amateur and played on Curtis Cup teams in 1936 and '38 before turning pro in 1940 to represent Wilson. Betty Hicks turned pro after winning the 1941 Amateur.

Hope Seignious was from Greensboro and was the first woman golfer to act on creating some form of competitive tour for women pros. She founded the Women's Professional Golf Association in 1944 and copyrighted the name. Hope's father was a cotton broker, and she used her own money to organize the group. I believe she also published the first women's golf magazine. It failed and Bob Harlow bought her mailing list when he started his *Golf World* magazine in Pinehurst. Early WPGA members included Betty Hicks, Betty Jameson, Kathryn Hemphill and Ellen Griffin, a woman who would become very special to me in my career and have a strong influence over my interest in teaching golf.

Ellen was never a top player at the tournament level but was a trailblazer in golf instruction and the early promotion of women's golf. She taught physical education for twenty-eight years in Greensboro at the Woman's College of the University of North Carolina (now UNC-Greensboro) and later would help us create golf schools and "Golfaris" at Pine Needles. She spent many nights on the road, barnstorming from coast-to-coast to speak to college and high-school teachers on how to teach golf.

Hope ran the WPGA out of an office in the old Dixie Building in Greensboro, and her first order of business was to create a National Open. It was held in 1946 in a match-play format at Spokane Country Club and sponsored by the Spokane Athletic Round Table, a men's fraternal organization (the gentlemen contributed some of the purse for the Open from their slot machine proceeds). Patty won the first Open, beating Betty Jameson five-and-four in the final. I didn't play that year because Spokane was too far to travel for an amateur.

Because of their local ties to Greensboro, Hope and Ellen arranged to have the next Open in their backyard at Starmount Forest Country Club in Greensboro. Thirty-nine players — ten pros competing for $7,500 and twenty-nine amateurs —

played in the championship. The women hardly got any breaks in playing short courses back then, and the course played 6,524 yards, par-seventy-six. It wasn't until years later that organizers figured out that people like to see pros make birdies rather than struggle for pars and thus shortened the courses. My best round was a four-under seventy-two on Saturday, which set the course record for women, and finished eleven strokes behind the champion, Betty Jameson. I would have won about $800 after finishing in the top third of the field if I'd been a pro.

In 1948, there were only nine tournaments for women pro golfers, and the leading money-winner was Babe Zaharias, who raked in $3,400. It was during this period that Babe and her manager, Fred Corcoran, began to get serious about expanding the opportunities for women's pro golf.

After winning two gold medals and one silver in the 1932 Los Angeles Olympics, Babe turned to golf and by 1935 was ready to take on the somewhat limited options that amateur golf afforded. She won one of her first big tournaments, the state championship of the Women's Texas Golf Association, but her victory rankled certain factions in golf's establishment. She eventually lost her amateur status because she'd innocently accepted a free automobile from Chrysler. So for nearly ten years — until she eventually was reinstated and the amateur tour returned to normalcy after World War II — her outlets for competition were severely limited. In the meantime, she'd married George Zaharias. George was now a wrestling promoter, and he wanted Babe to get her amateur status back so she could become a champion golfer. He stayed busy promoting Babe until she turned professional again.

When Babe got her opportunity, she made the best of it, winning seventeen tournaments over the 1946 and 1947 seasons, culminating with the first-ever win for an American in the British Women's Amateur. At that point, the money was too enticing and Babe signed on with Corcoran to be her manager. She was now a professional for good.

Corcoran was manager of the PGA Tournament Bureau from 1937-48, then left the tour to manage individual athletes and pursue other sports enterprises. Amid efforts on behalf of high-profile clients like baseball greats Stan Musial and Ted Williams and men's golf star Sam Snead, Corcoran set up exhibition matches and clinics for Babe. But there simply weren't enough competitive opportunities for Babe, so she, Fred and her husband George realized they needed to create some.

That led to a meeting in January, 1949, at the Venetian Hotel in Miami that included Patty, Fred, Babe and George. They agreed to create a loosely organized tour that Corcoran would manage. Wilson Sporting Goods would pay the administrative costs for the tour. Before long, they got Spalding and MacGregor, the other two major equipment manufacturers, to help pay the bills as well.

Fred and Babe both thought "ladies" would sound better than "women's," plus Hope had the copyright on WPGA. So they decided the new organization would be called the Ladies Professional Golf Association. Articles of incorporation were agreed upon in 1950 at a pros-only meeting at the Women's Open in Wichita, Kansas. The women in that meeting are considered to be the official "founders" of the LPGA Tour. I was still an amateur that summer, so I wasn't in the meeting. Thus I am not a "founder" of the LPGA Tour, despite frequent designations in the press. The LPGA officially considers me a "pioneer" member. (To further complicate the matter, after turning professional in the fall of 1950, my LPGA membership card designated me a "Charter Member.")

Money was tight in those early days. Fred once said that while potential sponsors were polite when he called, he could "hear them stifling a yawn at the other end." There were no funds for tour staff, so we handled the day-to-day operations ourselves. One player would keep the books and write the checks and another handled the mail. We were our own officials; sometimes we'd have to make rulings on players we were competing against.

No one was getting rich, I assure you. We had fourteen events that first year, with $50,000 in prize money, an average of three to four grand per event, with the winner getting about fifteen percent. I can remember some with only a $1,500 purse. We supplemented our prize money with clinics and exhibitions; only in those days, we were just trying to break even. We weren't making a fortune like pros do today with Monday exhibitions. Lots of players shared expenses and traveled together. I won only $2,175 in 1951. By 1953, there were twenty-four events, and Louise Suggs banked $19,816 to lead the money list. Babe, Patty, Louise and Betty Jameson were the best players on tour at the time.

My first professional event was the Ponte Vedra Open, held in January, 1951. The purse was $3,000. The local newspaper said I was the "sentimental favorite since it was my first pro event since leaving the simon-pure ranks." During the tournament, a representative of the Ponte Vedra Inn & Golf Club asked if I'd like to represent the inn on tour. They paid me $1,000 a year, and between tournaments I'd return to Ponte Vedra, enjoy the inn and play golf with their guests. I continued that relationship through the 1953 season, until I married Bullet and we acquired Pine Needles.

Spalding made Peggy Kirk Clubs for Women, with two woods selling for $19 and five irons for $36. After I married Bullet in 1953, I insisted they change the name on the clubs to Peggy Kirk Bell. I can't tell you how many women have come up to me over the years — many of them visitors at Pine Needles — and told me their first set of clubs was one of mine.

Occasionally an opportunity to do an exhibition tour came along. One I remember best came in 1953 when Marlene and Alice Bauer, Jackie Pung and I took a five-week tour of Australia. It was sponsored by the country's biggest oil company, Ampol Oil. They paid each of us $3,000 plus expenses to come over, but they asked us to take some or all of the payment in Ampol stock since it was difficult to get dollars out of the Australia at the time. Jackie said she was building a house and needed all her money in cash. The Bauer sisters' father was running their interests and said they had to bring it all home. So I told the man, "Pay me a thousand and put two thousand in stock." A few months later, they struck oil in Perth and that $1 stock shot to $70 a share! It eventually fell back some but I still made a nice return.

One of the interesting things about that trip was that we got to meet Richard Nixon. The newly elected vice-president to Dwight Eisenhower was on a world tour and had visited the Australian prime minister in Sydney. Thousands of people were lined up to meet him one day, and our hosts arranged for us to go to the head of the line and shake hands and speak with him and his wife, Pat. He thanked us for representing the United States through golf.

The All-American and World Championship at Tam O'Shanter in Chicago were the biggest tournaments of the year and all of us looked forward to playing them. They had the largest purse and had competition for women pros and amateurs and men pros and amateurs. They had huge crowds and were the first tournaments to build spectator bleachers around greens and tees. George May, who ran the tournament, was quite a man. He'd sit by the first tee and say, "Peggy, what do you think you're going to shoot today?"

I might say, "George, I feel like about a seventy-eight."

He'd say, "Okay, shoot that and you win a hundred bucks." After your round, if you'd made your target, you'd go to his office and he'd peel off a $100 bill and give it to you. And he was happy. He wanted to lose! He liked helping the golfers.

The courses the LPGA was playing then were longer and not nearly in the kind of condition today's courses are. We always played from the middle of the men's tee on the first day of a tournament, then we'd move three-quarters of the way back, then all the way back. Some of the players wanted to use shorter tees, but Babe would have nothing to do with that. So we all learned to play these long, long courses. They were much longer than the 6,300 yards Pine Needles was set up for in the 1996 Women's Open. One course measured 6,900 yards. But Babe knew that the longer the course, the more advantage she had. Half the four-pars were drivers from the tee and woods or long-irons into the greens for us. If we had a hole of 350 yards, that was a real birdie hole.

Because of the length of the courses, we worked long and hard to develop good short games. You were going to miss a bunch of greens every round, and getting up-and-down could be the key to your career. Even today the average player can get a good lesson in the importance of the short game by following the LPGA Tour. Colleen Walker once had nineteen chip-ins during one year on tour! It wasn't until Babe passed away and Lenny Wirtz became LPGA commissioner in the 1960s that the courses we played became more reasonable in length. They figured that people would be more inclined to come watch golfers shoot low scores than struggle to break par.

The only part of tour life that really got to me was all the driving. The tour would start in the winter in and around Florida — starting in Sea Island, going to Tampa, Havana (before Castro), Miami Beach, St. Petersburg, Sarasota, Jacksonville and Augusta — and then cross the country to New Orleans, Texas, Phoenix, Las Vegas and into California. You'd put as much as 40,000 miles on your car a year, and you were driving mostly two-lane roads without all the service amenities we have on the highway today. The good thing was that back then we all drove big cars that had plenty of trunk space for our clothes. Patty always rode the train. Wiffi Smith first traveled in a 1928 Ford A Model, but later switched to a VW Van with a full-sized piano, which she played to strengthen her fingers after she had broken her hands in a motorcycle accident.

Eventually I found a way out of all the driving. The world of airplanes and flying had fascinated me since childhood, and during World War II, I wanted to go into the Women's Air Force Services. I thought it would be great to learn to fly at the government's expense. But I was rejected because I'm red-green color blind. I did, however, serve in the Civil Air Patrol during the war in hopes of learning to fly. We got through ground school and marched in parades, but the war ended before we actually learned to fly.

The golf tour was in New Orleans in 1952 and I was moaning to Gloria Armstrong, an amateur from California, about loathing the next drive across the country to California.

"If I were a pro, I'd fly from tournament to tournament," said Gloria, who had a pilot's license and even owned her own Stinson airplane. "Say, Peggy, why don't you buy a plane and I'll teach you to fly as you go to California?"

"Now *that* would be fun," I said.

Gloria taught me a lot about flying as we headed west and helped me buy my airplane, a Cessna 170 that cost $8,000 at a dealership in Dallas. I flew around the golf tour coast-to-coast for the next eight years and, after my eldest daughter Bonnie's birth in 1954, I sometimes took Bonnie and her nursemaid. Babe was a frequent travel partner as well. I made a lot of friends among fellow pilots, and we even held the first Pilots National Golf Championship at Pine Needles in 1955. Entrants had to have a valid pilot's license to play in the thirty-six-hole tournament, and most of them were airline pilots. The winner was the vaunted amateur golfer, Frank Stranahan, of Toledo, Ohio.

I had several harrowing experiences, the last of which grounded me for good. I was flying from Findlay to Southern Pines in 1959 when a snowstorm moved in. Snow severely limits your vision — you can only see straight down. I had to fly low and use a railroad for navigation as I flew over Virginia. I was scared to death. I said a big prayer that afternoon, desperately wanting to make it home to Bullet and our two little girls (Peggy Ann had been born in 1958). "God, if you get me down safely, I promise I'll sell this plane," I prayed.

Eventually, below my left wing, I saw an open field, did a 180-degree turn and landed the plane. I kept my word. I sold the plane and used the proceeds to build the swimming pool at Pine Needles. To this day, every time I go past that pool I think of my plane!

As soon as we arrived in a new town, we had to catch up on laundry and do rounds of the radio stations and newspapers to drum up publicity for that week's tournament. The existence of our tour depended on healthy gate receipts, so public relations was always a priority with us. And there was always a reception or luncheon to attend with the local organizers and club members. In Cincinnati, St. Louis and New York, some of us would go to baseball games and Babe would hit golf balls from home plate into the outfield as a promotion for the tournament. Once things settled down in the evenings, we'd listen to the radio, play cards and write letters. Appearance was very important. We knew we needed to look good, down to having our shoes polished.

The Titleholders in Augusta was probably the most popular tournament. One of the highlights was a talent show called "Fun Night"; among the stars would be Babe on her harmonica, the Bauer sisters singing, Patty's imitation of the worst golf swings, Jackie's hula dance and Betty Dodd's guitar. The rest of us would play parts in skits.

By 1959, the LPGA had twenty-six tournaments and $200,000 in prize money. When Babe died in 1956, the tour suffered a lapse of momentum, but Mickey Wright came along and was one of the big attractions in the 1960s. A lot of us say Mickey was the greatest women's golfer of all time. She had a pure swing — great fundamentals, wonderful rhythm, terrific power and precision. People came to see a show with Babe. They came to see a great swing and great golf with Mickey. She won four U.S. Opens, four LPGA Championships and two Titleholders — a total of eighty-two tournaments overall.

As the 1960s evolved, I averaged playing around a dozen tournaments a year. In 1963, I played in eleven events and won only $673, averaging seventy-nine strokes over thirty-five rounds and finishing thirty-sixth on the money list. Two years later, Bullet had the first of a long series of heart attacks, and with three young children (Kirk was born in 1962), a busy resort and a growing golf instruction business, I played fewer and fewer events. Mainly I just played in the major tournaments each year.

Competitive golf was not my priority when the game began undergoing major changes in the 1970s. But it was nice to watch them from the periphery and see women's golf begin to evolve into a place it deserved. The key changes included new marketing opportunities, the landing of Nancy Lopez as a new star and the across-the-board new opportunities for women in athletics.

Corporate sponsorship grew as the women's tour became more popular. Alvin Handmacher, whose company made Weathervane suits for women, was one of the early supporters of the tour. His backing created the Weathervane Tour, a series of four, thirty-six hole tournaments held in various cities across the country from 1950-53 and paying $3,000 each. In those cities we went to stores like Neimen Marcus and modeled their suits. Sirbin Golf Dress out of Miami was also one of the early sponsors of LPGA tournaments. The company signed Babe Zaharias, so a lot of us got all the Sirbin dresses we wanted. Sears, Roebuck & Company was another business that saw vast potential in the marketing value of supporting women's golf. It spent a lot of money in golf equipment, especially on ladies clubs in the 1950s. Spalding made Peggy Kirk clubs that were sold through Sears, and I used to make regular appearances at Sears stores around the country where I'd hit balls into a net set up in the store or sometimes even in the parking lot. For 50 years Spalding has been very good to me. They sponsor the Peggy Kirk Bell-Rollins College Intercollegiate Golf Tournament.

Corporate sponsorship grew to a new level in the 1970s with the involvement of the Colgate-Palmolive Company, and its chairman, David Foster. Colgate made dozens of household products and Foster, an avid golfer, believed that courting women through pro golf was a smart promotional play. Foster created the Colgate-Dinah Shore Winner's Circle tournament, which was held in Palm Springs, California, and it became one of the biggest events annually on the LPGA Tour. In fact, it became a major because the prize money was the largest on tour.

The tour produced a variety of stars and superstars who, after Babe's death in 1956, followed in her footsteps. Mickey Wright was one; she had the best swing I'd ever seen on tour. Judy Rankin was the first woman to win more than $100,000 in a season and was paid huge promotional dollars by Colgate. Kathy Whitworth and JoAnne Carner won lots of majors and plenty of money. Kathy was a sweet person and a great champion. She was a good enough friend to host my golf school when I went on one of the European cruises. She was a lot of fun and the students really loved having this great champion. She won eighty-eight tournaments, more than any woman or man in the history of golf.

The arrival of Nancy Lopez as a nine-time winner on the 1978 tour signaled yet another milestone. Her smiling, healthy face graced the cover of *Sports Illustrated*. Galleries gravitated to her vivacious personality. She was a great golfer and had a lot of fun playing and winning, which attracted fans, sponsors and television. The media cornered her every week. She was besieged by autograph hounds.

Tournament officials prayed for her to enter their events. It was a 1970s-version of the "Tigermania" we've seen recently on the PGA Tour. Over the next few years, she would attract attention, interest and dollars to the game. Overall, LPGA purses increased from a total of $600,000 in 1970 to $4 million in 1979, thanks in part to David Foster and Nancy Lopez. The 2001 Tour is playing for $43.5 million.

In 2000, I played with Nancy in a grand opening of a course in Wisconsin named Horseshoe Bay, and she remains an immensely popular and congenial personality in golf. She signed a lot of autographs that day and has never turned down an autograph request. Once as a child, she stood in line for what seemed to her like hours to get the autograph of a big-name golf star. When her time had finally come at the head of the line, the golfer said, "That's it, no more signing," and turned around and left. Nancy cried and cried and cried. She vowed that day that if ever anyone wanted her autograph, she'd not leave until the last person was accommodated.

During the 1970s, another important societal change was taking place. I grew up in an era where there were few opportunities for girls to play interscholastic or intercollegiate athletics. We played intramurals and that was it. The federal government ruled in the early 1970s through Title IX that women should be extended the same opportunities as men for athletic competition, and slowly more girls played more sports at an earlier age.

When my daughter Bonnie entered the University of North Carolina in 1976 after two years at St. Mary's College in Raleigh and one at Rollins College, my alma mater, the Carolina women's golf program was in its infancy. I'd taught golf to Sally Austin, a young lady who grew up in nearby Raeford, North Carolina. When she entered UNC in 1973, there was no women's golf program. So Sally and her dad talked to the athletic director, Homer Rice, and the former athletic director, Chuck Erickson, who was serving as a consultant to the athletic department, and asked if the university would start a women's golf team. They were receptive to the idea, and Homer sent out a recruiting letter. Soon the program got started with Sally and three other young ladies, though no scholarships were given at the time. One of the original golfers, Mindy Moore, played the LPGA Tour and would later join the staff of the LPGA and is director of player/sponsor relations.

Two decades later, Sally returned to UNC as the new women's golf coach, replacing Dot Gunnells, and today she has six full scholarships and a database of thousands of junior golfers to recruit. The growth of the game has been phenomenal.

I look on the changes in the game with mixed emotions. The opportunity and money is there today for young girls in golf. I'm glad for that, but the personality of the old amateur tour that I clung to before turning pro is now just a distant memory.

CHAPTER 5
My Friend, The Babe

Babe Didrikson Zaharias was full of surprises from the first moment our lives crossed in 1945. From that day forward, I would never be shocked at any thing she said or did.

We were at the Women's Western Open in Chicago that summer. Babe had reached the finals and received word that her mother had died. I assumed she would withdraw and go home. I certainly would have. But Babe vowed to win the tournament for her mother. And she did.

Two years later, I got a call from Babe.

"I need a partner for the Women's International Four-Ball," she said, "and you might as well win a tournament."

I met her in Hollywood, Florida, for the tournament, and I was very nervous the day of the first round. She could sense that I was on edge, and she told me to relax. "I can beat any two of them without you," she said. "I'll let you know if I need you." Of course, we won the tournament.

And thus we were off on a friendship that provided a life full of memories. Babe would become the leading force behind the formation of the LPGA Tour. She was the most outstanding woman athlete of her day — perhaps of all time. She was funny and outrageous and powerful and talented. And I had a front-row seat for every step of the journey.

Babe was one of seven children of a Norwegian ship carpenter who had immigrated to Port Arthur, Texas. She grew up in Beaumont and was the quintessential tomboy. She picked up her nickname after she hit five home runs once in a baseball game while playing on her older brother's team, and she was the star on the Beaumont High girls' basketball team.

Babe was only eighteen years old when the 1932 Olympics were held in Los Angeles. She won gold medals in the eighty-meter hurdles and the javelin throw and a silver in the high jump. She could easily have won more gold. But her first place in the high jump was disqualified because she went over head first — known as the "Western roll" and the precursor to the standard technique today — and women couldn't enter more than three events. She could have competed in the discus or the sprints or long distances and won more medals. Babe was asked by a reporter if there was anything she didn't play, and she answered, "Yeah, dolls."

Up to that time, Babe had played only a few rounds of casual golf. She had become a media darling at the Olympics, and several sportswriters, including the famed Grantland Rice, enticed her onto the course at Brentwood Country Club the day after the Olympics concluded. Rice was a big fan of Babe and told her she could be good at the game. Babe amazed them with her towering drives; she reached the apron of the 523-yard seventeeth in two shots. She was so good simply because she was so athletic; Rice later mused that if she'd starting playing golf as a kid, there was no telling how great she would have been. Later, after watching Bobby Jones in an exhibition match, Babe's desire to learn golf and become a great player was ignited.

The world of golf would never be the same.

Babe hit a thousand balls a day for more than a year and sometimes practiced sixteen hours a day. In the fall of 1934, she entered her first tournament and shot a seventy-seven to win the medal in the Fort Worth Invitational before being eliminated in an early round of match play. She kept working on her game and the following spring won the state championship of the Women's Texas Golf Association

For all her fame and glory, life wasn't always easy for Babe, particularly in her early days in golf. She came from a working-class family and had three brothers and two sisters. Some people didn't think she fit in the world of golf, and at times she was snubbed and ostracized. Right after she won in Texas, there was a movement among some rivals to have the United States Golf Association declare her a professional. In 1935, Babe was given an automobile by the Chrysler Motor Co., which unknowingly made her a professional. So for eleven years, Babe didn't have any tournaments to play except the Western Open, the Texas Open and assorted other open events like the Los Angeles Open.

It was at the L.A. Open in 1938 when she met her husband, pro wrestler George Zaharias. Babe, George and a Presbyterian minister were grouped together for the first two rounds, and Babe and George took an immediate liking to each other. Photographers asked them to mug for the cameras on the first tee, and George grabbed Babe in playful wrestling holds. After the second round, George invited Babe to his place for dinner, and from then on they were an item. They married in December.

After she was ruled a professional, Babe signed with Goldsmith Sporting Goods to do a tour of exhibitions with Gene Sarazen. Marrying George, however, altered her reliance on the money she was making doing exhibitions and sponsorships. George was a successful pro wrestler and had plenty of money, freeing Babe to do the thing she loved most — compete on the golf course. She applied to the USGA for reinstatement as an amateur in January, 1940, but there was a three-year probationary period before she could regain her amateur status. By that time, the golf world had ground to a near standstill until the completion of World War II.

When the war was over in 1945 and the amateur circuit got back into full swing, Babe shot off like a cannon. She won seventeen tournaments over two years, stumbling only in the inaugural Women's National Open, held in Spokane, Washington, in 1946. Among her victories were the 1946 U.S. Women's Amateur and in 1947 she was the first American to win the British Women's Amateur. Then in 1947, after winning the British Amateur, she accepted $300,000 from a film producer for a series of golf programs and now was voluntarily and officially a professional. Fred Corcoran became her manager and began getting her $1,000 for golf exhibitions — the same price commanded by Ben Hogan and Sam Snead.

From that point on, Babe was influential in getting tournaments started for all of us and eventually in the formation of the LPGA. I remember sitting in hotel rooms and listening as Babe negotiated over the phone with tournament organizers — turning what could have been an exhibition for her into a tournament for her and the rest of us. They'd offer her a $1,000 for the appearance, so she'd say, "I'll tell you what. You put up $500 more, and I'll come and bring the girls with me." And all of a sudden, you've got a tournament with a $1,500 purse.

People remember Babe for her astonishing length, and there's no question she could crunch the golf ball. Once Babe was playing an exhibition with Snead. They were playing from the same tees, and Babe outdrove Sam on one hole. He accused her of playing with a souped-up ball. What was truly amazing was that Babe was not a large woman — in fact, she stood only five feet, six and a half inches tall.

Babe started with a long, loopy, John Daly-type swing and had no idea where it was going. One drive was measured at 409 yards. She had one of the most perfect, relaxed grips. She came through impact so fast that she recoiled like firing a shotgun. She later developed a shorter, more upright swing like Byron Nelson's. Babe used to say, "I loosen my girdle and let it fly." The fact was, she didn't even wear a girdle. But people loved to hear her say it.

We all had our own shag bag filled with the brand of golf balls we played. I remember our caddies would use baseball gloves to field our practice shots. Babe's caddie would stand out there on range and catch iron shot after iron shot, rarely moving more than a step to catch the ball. Her woods traveled longer distances, of course, and weren't always as straight as the irons.

But there was a lot more to her game than power. She was a great wedge player and developed an excellent touch around the greens. She could make dozens of five-footers in a row, despite a somewhat unorthodox putting style that had her flexed left elbow pointed at the target.

Babe was exactly what women's golf needed at the time — a dominant force and personality to rally around. Our game grew because of her flair and color and her great distance. Patty Berg used to say that "Babe put the power into the swing," and that was when everyone thought we should swing like a lady instead of an athlete.

There was never a dull moment around Babe; she was just an overgrown kid. She loved practical jokes. We were staying in a member's home during a tournament in Orlando when George had returned to California on business. I came out of the bathroom, and it looked like she was asleep in the other bed. Actually she'd stuffed pillows under the covers and was hiding under my bed. I turned out the lights, started to crawl into my bed, and she grabbed my foot. I screamed and jumped three feet. Another time we were sharing a room and I thought she was asleep in the other bed. Babe had tied a string to my springs and just when I dozed off, she pulled the string from my bed and woke me up. I looked over at her, and she seemed asleep. After another wake-up, she began to laugh.

People came out in droves to see Babe. We were partners in the 1947 Women's International Four-Ball at Orange Brook in Hollywood. Some 4,000 fans showed up for the thirty-six hole finals match against Louise Suggs and Jean Hopkins. Daylight was running out as we moved to the thirty-sixth tee, the match all square. My second shot tailed to the right but hit a spectator and bounced onto the green. Then Louise hit her tee shot and said she wouldn't play, that it was too dark, but Babe insisted we finish since we'd started the hole. We never should've started the 36th hole, it really was too dark. In the end, the tournament official ruled it was too dark to play and that we'd come back and play another eighteen the next day. Babe did show up the next day, and we won three-and-two in an eighteen-hole playoff. We never played the thirty-sixth hole from the previous day.

Babe had it all — a famous name, a knack for thriving in the spotlight, and a deft touch with sponsors and tournament organizers. She was the Walter Hagen or Lee Trevino of women's golf. She was entertaining to the galleries. She'd hit a good one and turn to the guys watching behind her. "Don't you fellows wish you could hit it like that?" she'd say. They really laughed. And she was a genius at using the press to further her cause and that of women's golf.

Once we were in Denver. She shot a seventy-eight in a practice round and the reporters came up after and said, "Babe, what'd you shoot?"

"Around seventy, I think," she said.

Later, I said, "Babe, you shot seventy-eight!"

"Well," she said, "it *could* have been a seventy. Besides, Peggy, they don't want to hear that I shot seventy-eight. I tell them what they want to hear." So the next day the headlines in the paper read "Babe Warms Up With 70."

Babe was always saying she could do this or that and then do it. One time we were playing a practice round at Dubsdread in Orlando, Florida, and came to the three-par twelfth hole, where she knocked a seven-iron into the hole. The next day, we came back to that hole. "They haven't moved the pin," she said. "I think I can do it again." And she did! She turned to the gallery and said, "I told you I could." Years later, when she was in the hospital, she finished a cigarette and pointed to an empty Coke bottle on the dresser across the room. "Bet I can flip it in that Coke bottle," she said. Of course, she flipped it, it bounced off the mirror and into the bottle — about a one in a million chance.

I remember sitting in a hotel room with George and Babe when a Hollywood director or a man who represented the movie *Pat and Mike* with Katherine Hepburn and Spencer Tracy came in. The director/representative wanted Babe to play a golf match with Katherine Hepburn where Katherine would win. Babe said "Count me out, I'm not going to lose to anyone even if it's for a movie." The man went back to Hollywood and rewrote the script so Babe would win, and she agreed to be in the movie.

Babe was named Woman Athlete of the Year several times, and one year she had just accepted the award in New York and was asked, "What are your plans?" She told everyone she was going to enter the men's U.S. Open the next year. Well, the reporters stormed out and it was all over the papers the next day: "Babe To Enter Men's U.S. Open." So the USGA called a special meeting and officially banned all women at that time from the men's Open. She was never serious in the first place but loved all the commotion it created. She loved to shock people.

Babe was my eldest daughter Bonnie's god-mother and told me just after her birth in 1954 that she assumed I'd name the baby after her.

"Name the baby 'Mildred?'" I said. "You don't even *like* 'Mildred.'"

"No, I mean 'Babe.' It'll look great in print: 'Babe Bell Wins The Open.'" She was always thinking of the press.

Bullet and I decided on Bonnie Kirk Bell. Of course, Babe said, "Bonnie Bell. That'll look good in print, too."

Babe was in Washington, D.C., speaking at a fundraiser for the Republican Party the day Bonnie was born. The President invited her to stay over, presumably to stay in the White House, but Babe said thanks but no, she had to get to Southern Pines to see her friend and her new baby. The next day Babe was up on the ward in the hospital, and she called John Hemmer, the famous photographer in Pinehurst, to come take a picture of her with the baby and doctor. Bullet called from the golf shop and said Ike's office had just called, trying to get Babe. So Babe called the White House from my room in the hospital. I remember the operator telling Babe she couldn't just call the President's office like that, and Babe retorting, "Why not? He just tried to call me!" It turns out his office wanted Babe to reread part of the speech she'd given because it had been obscured by ovations and laughter.

You just never knew what would come out of Babe's mouth. One night George, Babe, my father and I were having dinner and a gentleman approached very politely and said, "Mrs. Zaharias, I hate to disturb your dinner, but my friends and I have a bet on how far you threw the javelin in the Olympics."

Babe hardly acknowledged the man but said, "Farther than anyone else in the world." The poor man almost crawled back to his table. We were shocked and told her to go apologize. She planned to all along.

She said, "I'm going to have some fun." So she walked over, pulled up a chair and said, "Okay, let's talk about me for a while." She must have spent half an hour entertaining those men.

For Babe to have the athletic ability and that unique personality would have been enough to create a dozen superstars. But what really made her one of a kind were her talents in other areas. She was a terrific musician, particularly with the harmonica. Name her a tune and she could play it. She'd performed Vaudeville before taking up golf seriously and was on *The Ed Sullivan Show*. She was outstanding in basketball and baseball. She would beat you at tennis, marbles and swimming. She was a great cook (she had two ovens in her kitchen), a fast and accurate typist, a talented seamstress. She'd be ironing a blouse and say, "I'm the best ironer there is." And she probably was.

Babe was in New York one year in the early 1950s to do *The Ed Sullivan Show*. She was going to play the harmonica and Betty Dodd the guitar. They were walking down Fifth Avenue and came to a jewelry store. Babe looked in the window and saw a ladies' Rolex watch, the first of the ladies' line. She went in the store, asked to see a phone book and looked up the address for the Rolex corporate headquarters. She got the address, and they jumped in a cab and went to the Rolex headquarters.

Babe walked into the administrative office and the secretary asked, "What can I do for you?"

Babe told her, "Tell the president Babe Didrikson Zaharias is here and would like to see him."

The secretary grudgingly obliged, not knowing who this audacious woman was. A minute later, the president came out, grinning from ear-to-ear and welcomed her with open arms and asked, "What can I do for you, Babe?"

"I have got to have one of those new ladies' Rolexes," she told the man.

The president knew a good PR stunt when he saw one. "Okay, we'll go to Toots Shore's for lunch, have a press conference and I'll present you with a Rolex. Then we'll go to Winged Foot and play eighteen holes."

Babe's reply was, "George needs one, too."

So Babe got two Rolex watches. A lot of people believe Arnold Palmer was the first golfer to wear a Rolex. But Babe beat him to it.

In 1951, Fred Corcoran arranged for a tour of England for six of us — Babe, Patty, Betsy Rawls, Betty Jameson, Betty Bush and I. It was called the Weathervane Team, and it was the first women's professional team to tour England. We played a series against Britain's best women, but Fred also arranged a match against six male players from their former Walker Cup teams. One of their players was Leonard Crawley, the former team captain and at the time the golf editor of the *London Daily Telegraph and Morning Mail*. Leonard's trademark was a long, elegant handlebar mustache.

Crawley said he wanted to play with Babe, so of course Babe was primed for the challenge. On the first tee, Crawley said, "Now Mildred, you play from the women's tees."

Babe said, "No way. I'm going to play back here and hit with you, Leonard."

Babe wanted to play for something, so she said, loud enough for the gallery to hear, "If I beat you, I want you to shave off that mustache." Crawley agreed, thinking there was no way he'd lose to a woman.

Of course, Babe won, two-and-one. Crawley was so mad he stormed off the course and left. Babe was later seen running around the parking lot with a pair of scissors, looking for Crawley.

Babe had her detractors because of her domineering ways, and I admit I could see how she could rub some people the wrong way. She used to say, "I wish these girls would play better. Then I'd have to practice." Some golfers took exception to Babe's boasting and sometimes overbearing personality, but everyone respected her and knew that she was the main draw to women's golf. She could get way with her remarks, because most of it was her just kidding around. She loved to make people laugh.

I remember once in a players' meeting, someone complained about Babe receiving appearance money at tournaments. Babe was quick with a response. "I'm the star of this show and all of you are in the chorus," she said. "I receive some money and if it weren't for me, half of our tournaments wouldn't have a purse and wouldn't even be."

Afterward I told her, "Babe, you shouldn't have said that. I could have explained it better by telling them how people called you to give an exhibition and you talked them into putting up another $500 for a tournament, that was how the LPGA got some of its earlier tournaments." But she was right. And that was The Babe. She was totally honest and said what she thought.

But she had another side as well in looking out for the other golfers. Dick Taylor, the long-time editor of *Golf World* magazine, remembers at the Breakers Hotel in Palm Beach when Babe demanded that her fellow competitors be moved from the "servants quarters," as she called them, into standard guest rooms like the one she had. Babe threatened to withdraw from the tournament if they weren't moved. Of course, the other girls were moved.

Babe wound up winning forty-one professional tournaments, including thirty-one after the LPGA was officially formed in 1950. There's no telling how many tournaments Babe might have won had it not been for the cancer that eventually took her life in 1956.

She first encountered health problems in 1952; that turned out to be a hernia that was surgically removed. Then late that year, she started feeling tired all the time. She never really regained her strength. When the 1953 spring tour moved to her hometown in Beaumont for the Babe Zaharias Open, she visited her longtime physician. She was diagnosed with cancer and within a week, Babe was in surgery and had a colostomy.

Babe came back and won the 1954 U.S. Women's Open, a minor miracle given the health problems she'd had. She beat Betty Hicks by twelve shots at Salem Country Club in Peabody, Mass. I had to withdraw from the championship because I was pregnant with Bonnie, and Babe called every night with a report. "I'm killin' 'em out here," she'd say. Afterwards she told the press: "My prayers have been answered. I wanted to show thousands of cancer sufferers that the operation I had will enable a person to return to a normal life. I have received 15,000 inquiries from those who have undergone the operation, and this is my answer to them."

In April, 1955, she won her last tournament, the Peach Blossom Classic in Spartanburg, S.C. In July she went back into the hospital and was in and out through September, 1956, when she died.

I still remember the last time we played golf together as if it were yesterday. It was sometime in

61

the early part of 1956 at Tampa Country Club (which Babe and George owned), and she was so weak because of the medication and the pain in her back that she was only driving the ball as far as I hit it. She couldn't even put on golf shoes. She just wore plain loafers.

The first hole was 305 yards, and Babe nearly always drove the green. This day she was way short of it. After about five holes, Babe said to me, "Peggy, you sure are a great golfer. How can you break eighty hitting it so short?" She was used to hitting an eight-iron when I was hitting a six-iron. The game had always been easy for her. That day she was in such pain that she could only play nine holes. She never played golf again.

When Babe died, the tour was never the same and dwindled for a while. Thanks to Patty Berg and Louise Suggs, the tour kept going; then it took off again when Mickey Wright came along.

Few people know that in September, 1981, Babe and Bob Jones were the first athletes of any sport to have a commemorative United States Postage Stamp printed in their honor. I was delighted to receive the stamp on her behalf at Pinehurst during the Hall of Fame Classic, a professional tournament held at No. 2 at the time.

I'll always treasure that decade of memories I got from Babe Zaharias. I used to try to talk her into talking more about the Olympics, but she never wanted to. "Golf is my game," she said. "It puts me with nice people."

Peggy Kirk Bell with her sister, Grace Strong, on her left and Judy Bell on her right.

Pat McGowan, son-in-law and former PGA Rookie of the Year, and director of golf at Pine Needles Learning Center.

Mrs. Bell with Annika Sorenstam, winner of the 1995 and 1996 U.S. Women's Open (Pine Needles).

Mrs. Bell accepting the coveted Bob Jones Award from Gene Howerdd, USGA Official.

U.S. Weathervane Team — Betty Bush, Betsy Rawls, Peggy Kirk Bell, Betty Jameson, Patty Berg, and Babe Didrikson Zaharias.

Peggy with George Zaharias and Babe Didrikson Zaharias.

Mrs. Bell and Supreme Court Justice Sandra Day O'Connor enjoy a golf outting at Pine Needles.

Peggy Kirk Bell with Gary Wiren and Ellen Griffin during the NGF seminar at Pine Needles.

The Cheap Shot Tournament in memory of Bullet Bell. Craig Stadler sits in his hole-in-one prize. (Left to Right) Phil Hancock, Vance Heafner, Mark Lye, Paul Azinger, Clarence Rose, Pat McGowan, Mike Donald, Morris Hatalsky, Bill Kratzert, Leonard Thompson, Tim Norris.

Mrs. Bell with Arnold Palmer and his wife Winnie during a visit to Pine Needles.

Peggy Kirk Bell with Bob Jones autographing his book.

Peggy and her future husband Bullet, who made Pine Needles what it is today.

Peggy Kirk Bell with children and their spouses at Pine Needles: (front) Peggy Ann Miller, Holly Bell, Bonnie McGowan; (back) Kelly Miller, Kirk Bell and Pat McGowan.

Mrs. Bell with Bullet arriving in their plane at the Moore County Airport, Southern Pines in 1953.

Past champions Peggy Kirk Bell, Mickey Wright, Louise Suggs, Patty Berg, Sandra Palmer, Marilynn Smith and Kathy Whitworth at the Titleholders Tournament in 1972 at Pine Needles.

Peggy with John Erickson, president of FCA, and Barbara Nicklaus.

Mrs. Bell with Jack Nicklaus, the greatest player in the game.

Leonard Schumutte, pro at Findlay Country Club, who taught Peggy Kirk Bell to play.

Mrs. Bell with Fielding Wallace, USGA president, receiving the Titleholders Cup in 1949.

Runners-up Jean Hopkins and Louise Suggs (L) pose with winners Peggy Kirk Bell and Babe Didrikson Zaharias at the 1947 Hollywood International Four-Ball.

Peggy Kirk Bell with her grandchildren (left to right): KellyAnn 8, Michael 10, Blair 15, Gracie 2, Melody 12, Scotti 4.

Mrs. Bell with long-time friend, the late Bing Crosby.

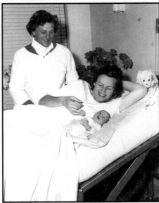

Peggy with newborn Bonnie and her godmother Babe Didrikson Zaharias.

CHAPTER 6
My Life In The Hotel Business

By the early 1950s my life had become relatively simple. I was enjoying traveling the country and playing professional golf. I had great friends in golf and had met a lot of fascinating people both home and abroad in my travels. I had a steady boyfriend, Bullet, though my travels and his job as a salesman for Spalding limited the time we could spend together.

Having just turned thirty, I knew deep down that a major decision was on the horizon. Do I stay single and continue the nomadic life of a professional golfer, or do I settle down, start a family and assume a more traditional lifestyle?

I had known Warren Bell since grade school in Findlay. There was a big stone quarry in town which was the kids' swimming hole, and he had a butch haircut and could swim underwater from one side to the other. The man who ran the place started calling him Bullet because of his speed boring through the water, and the nickname stuck forever.

Bullet was a three-time All-State basketball player and later went on to Ohio State. During World War II, he played on the All-Army team. After the war, he turned pro and signed with the Fort Wayne Pistons — today the Detroit Pistons. He had perfected a one-hand set shot after a shoulder injury in football limited the use of one shoulder. He was also a ball-handling whiz, so much so that one summer he filled in with the Harlem Globetrotters — after they painted his entire body black. A sportswriter came to up him later and said, "Bullet, I saw a guy playing for the Globetrotters who looked and played just like you!"

Bullet was a local celebrity in Findlay, and I was at home in May, 1946, after a winter of amateur golf. I stopped at a red light in my convertible and saw him standing on the corner.

"Hey, Kirkie," he said. "I hear you've been playing in some golf tournaments. You must be pretty good now. Bet I could beat you."

"You are kidding," I responded.

"We'll bet a movie," he said. "I win, you take me. You win, I take you." Bullet had a great personality and was a fun guy.

He was a great athlete but had never played golf. I beat him easily, and a leisurely courtship ensued. We had talked about marriage on occasion, but at that time it wasn't as proper for a woman to have a career and a family as well, and I didn't want to give up my golf career. Bullet insisted it was okay, I could keep playing the tour. But by 1953, he was ready to get on with his life. I loved him but was scared of the commitment. I finally agreed, and we set a date for August 15.

We planned a small service with only a few members of the immediate family present. I got cold feet at the last minute. I left town and went to the airport and jumped into my Cessna airplane for a ride and to think. You could lose yourself up there in the sky. The freedom is unlike anything else. I thought about it for three days and eventually called Bullet.

"Do you still want to get married?" I asked.

"Who is this?" he barked into the phone.

We were married that afternoon and joked for years that we had a pseudo-anniversary, August 15th, and a real one, August 18th.

Bullet knew little about golf when we played that first time in 1946, but over the next few years he learned to play and play well. His job calling on sporting goods stores in the Midwest for Spalding allowed him some time to play, and we would play when our schedules allowed. When we decided to get married and were thinking about where we'd live and what we'd do, we agreed that running — and preferably *owning* — a golf course would be ideal. So we both started investigating possible opportunities in that direction. We thought about building a course in Findlay. We also looked at several opportunities in Florida.

At one of the tournaments in Florida during the winter of 1953, I ran into some friends from Southern Pines, Maisie and Pop Cosgrove. The Cosgroves had been running Mid Pines Country Club in Southern Pines for eight years, and I had spent many wonderful times there with their daughter, Buttons, a good amateur golfer whom I'd met in the North and South Amateur years earlier.

Unfortunately, we all still ached from Buttons' tragic and untimely death just two years before. Buttons had met an amateur golfer named Julius Boros at Pinehurst in 1948, the year he tied Sam Snead for first in the North and South Open. Julius was known as "Jay" and was working for Mike Sherman at Southern Pines Country Club as an accountant before turning pro. They began courting and were married in 1950. Buttons gave birth to a son, Nicky, in the fall of 1951, but she died of a cerebral hemorrhage two days after Nicky's birth.

Jay had moved on with his life, and his golf career was blossoming. He won the 1952 U.S. Open, edging Ben Hogan, Sam Snead and Jimmy Demaret at Northwood Country Club in Dallas. But he and the Cosgroves were still close. I told Pop of our plans to get into the golf business, and he said he had an idea.

"You remember Pine Needles, across the street from us? It's been owned by the Catholic Church for five years," Pop said. "They don't want to run the golf course anymore. The course is for sale — $50,000 is the price. Let's buy it — Jay buys one-third, you and Bullet buy one-third, Maisie and I buy one-third. You and Jay keep playing golf, Maisie and I run Mid Pines, and Bullet can run Pine Needles."

Mid Pines and Pine Needles were created in the 1920s by the Tufts family of Pinehurst and a number of other investors. Business at Pinehurst had become so good that they believed a private club with guest accommodations (Mid Pines) and a resort hotel and residential community (Pine Needles) would be successful. Donald Ross designed both golf courses, and both were joys to play. Unfortunately, the Depression hit before either project could get a good head of steam and each was forced into bankruptcy. By the time Bullet and I came along, Pine Needles had been owned by the family of a noted amateur golfer George Dunlap Jr. The Air Force took it over in World War II and it was sold to the Roman Catholic Diocese of Raleigh, which planned to use it as a hospital.

It didn't take us long to decide it was a great situation. I sold some land in Findlay that I'd inherited, and Bullet cashed some life insurance. We pooled our resources for our $20,000 share. The Cosgroves put up $15,000 and Jay, the pro tour's leading money-winner in 1952 with just over $37,000, put up $15,000. We were now officially in the golf business.

The golf course we bought was in bad shape. Most of the grass on the fairways had not been fertilized. Rain had cut ruts all over the course. The greens were patchy and bumpy. Little scrawny scrub oaks and pines were all over the rough areas; if you hit your ball out of the fairway, you were likely to loose it in the trees and leaves. Bullet and Pop Cosgrove immediately set to work cleaning the course up and getting it in good condition. Green fees to play at Pine Needles were $1.50 and Bullet raised the fee to $2. "No one will pay $2 to play golf," I said. A few years later when he raised it to $3, I told him, "You just priced us out of business."

The golf course came with a five-year lease on a clubhouse that stood beside the original first tee (today the eighteenth) as well as barracks built by the Army Air Force that stood a hundred yards or so away. Today the barracks are gone, but the clubhouse building remains (you can see it to the left of the first fairway or behind the shrubs along the eighteenth tee) and is used as administrative offices for St. Joseph's of the Pines. "The Golfery," as the barracks were called, could hold about fifty men, paying $15 a day for room, board and golf. The men really roughed it in the barracks — they slept on Army cots, often went without hot water, and had to let us know when the roof leaked.

Weekends were the busy times. Golfers would board a train from the north after work Thursday, travel all night, and we'd meet them in our two station wagons and a truck at the Southern Pines depot at 7:00 a.m. Friday. The guests played golf all day Friday, Saturday and Sunday and would gather around the dinner table each evening for a family-style meal. We served an early dinner on Sunday and put them on the train at 7:30 p.m., so they could get back north in time for work Monday morning. It wasn't fancy, but the men enjoyed themselves, and we started to develop a good following.

Then came the first of a series of business challenges that would confront us over the years in the evolution of what we have today. In 1955, the Cosgroves and Jay wanted their money out of Pine Needles.

Mid Pines had been owned since 1934 by a Durham business, Homeland Investment Company. But Homeland wanted out of the resort business and offered to sell the resort to the Cosgroves, their long-time managers. In order for Pop and Maisie to raise the funds to buy Mid Pines, they needed their money out of Pine Needles — plus a nice little profit. Maisie told us she, Pop and Jay wanted $60,000 for their shares of Pine Needles.

"But you only put $30,000 into it two years ago," Bullet said.

"I know," Maisie said. "But that's what we've got to have. And we've got someone who'll pay it."

Bullet and I absolutely didn't want someone we didn't know buying into Pine Needles. But we didn't have the money ourselves. So we had to do something we didn't want to do — ask my father for a loan. Dad had been trying for two years to talk us into coming back to Findlay and taking over his wholesale grocery business. Now he tried again. But we told him our hearts were in golf.

"If your minds are made up, I'll help you," he said.

So we bought out the Cosgroves and Jay and now the Pine Needles golf course was ours.

Two years later brought our next major hurdle.

The lease for the Army barracks was up, and the church was firm on not wanting to extend it. So here we were with a golf course in a resort community and the prospect rapidly arising of having no place to house the golfers (and there was just one motel on Route 1). We needed a loan to build lodging facilities of our own.

Bullet carefully surveyed the property surrounding the golf course and believed that a strip of land running alongside Midland Road (the route between Southern Pines and Pinehurst) would be the ideal spot for our lodging operations. We were able to buy the land for $20,000. He designed a series of four five-bedroom lodges that would sit on the hillside, overlooking the course. At the time, the course started from the old inn on what is now the eighteenth hole. The current first was the original second, and so on around the course. Bullet's plan was to start the course on the old second hole and headquarter our operation on the south side of the property. Bullet had studied mechanical drawing in high school and drew the plans for the new buildings himself.

We needed $100,000 — a lot of money at the time. We thought we'd be able to get the money with no problem. We had a good, loyal clientele. There were no liens on the golf course. But Bullet talked to the only bank in Southern Pines, and they turned him down. I said I'd give it a try. They turned me down as well. I came out of the bank and met Bullet and I can remember like it was yesterday, standing on that street corner in Southern Pines, commiserating over our problems.

I like to believe that there are no coincidences, that everything happens for a reason and is part of God's plan. So I have no doubt that God sent a man named Jimmy Hobbs down the street to find us that day, so crestfallen and desperate. Jimmy was in the insurance business and was a casual friend of ours. He asked what the problem was, and we told him.

Jimmy nodded his head. "I'll see if I can get you the money," he said and walked off.

"What was that all about?" I asked.

"He's just trying to cheer us up," Bullet said.

One week later, Hobbs called. "A man named Frank Houston of Occidental Life Insurance in Raleigh is coming down to meet you and play golf with you," he said. "He might be able to help with your problem."

Houston drove down to Southern Pines and we gave him a tour of the place and told him about our plans. He apparently was impressed. At day's end, he said, "I'll loan you the money."

Bullet was hoping to get the commitment in writing. "We've had a bunch of promises that fell through," he said.

"I'll call you tomorrow," Houston said.

And he did. It was a tremendous relief.

With that $100,000, we built the four lodges that stand to the right of the clubhouse as you look at them from the first tee — $20,000 for each five-room lodge and $5,000 more for furniture. Bullet had drawn the plans, and after the contractor raised his price at the last minute, Bullet figured he could hire all the sub-contractors himself and save the money. We had a lot of help from some great people. Bullet developed a relationship with a carpenter named John Newton. John worked at Pine Needles until he retired, assisting Bullet in adding about one building a year until Pine Needles was completed. Another man, Clyde Upchurch of Raeford, sold us the cement blocks and said, "Pay me when you can."

The next year, Bullet drew plans for a clubhouse, dining room, pro shop and locker rooms, and construction began in the summer of 1958. Our lease had expired on the "Golfery" June 1, and we had reservations for golfers beginning November 1. By mid-August, the clubhouse was running over budget and we were out of money to finish and furnish it.

"What do we do now?" Bullet wondered.

"I've got an idea," I said.

I drove to Pinehurst to the Carolina Bank, which had operated since 1914 (originally it was the Bank of Pinehurst). The bank served the employees and guests of Pinehurst Inc. as well as the village cottagers. And though it was independent from Pinehurst Inc., Richard Tufts was the bank president. I was a little scared that Pinehurst might look at us as competition and not give us the loan, but I

71

was wrong. Mr. Tufts said that any growth was good for the area. It was a wonderful gesture.

The money in hand, it was still a race to the opening of the season to finish the building. Bullet bet carpenters steak dinners they couldn't finish various parts by certain dates. The work moved quickly. When guests arrived in early November, they sat on one side of the dining room while hammers pounded and kitchen equipment was installed. The guests even helped unpack furniture. By November 3, the clubhouse was finished.

We created quite a stir around Southern Pines by painting the buildings brown with orange trim. The locals believed everything should be green and white, and we were seen as these Yankee carpetbaggers coming into town and ruining the place. But Bullet stood firm, as he always did if it was an issue he believed in. Even our famous and conservative friend, Herbert Warren Wind, the great golf writer, told us that the colors helped identify Pine Needles. He said he would never have picked brown and orange, but it was a smart thing to do. We have since given up the orange, and now the buildings are brown and tan.

The 1958-59 season dawned with us owning the entire facility — twenty rooms, clubhouse, dining room and golf course. Now we set about expanding each year with profits from the previous season and more money from the Carolina Bank. We got to seventy-four rooms and figured that was plenty. Most of our guests played thirty-six holes a day, so that insured uncrowded golf. Bullet used to say, "You are treated like a member when you stay at Pine Needles."

Along the way, we were innovators. We were the first golf course to have golf carts. Richard Tufts swore there'd never be a golf cart in Pinehurst. But we'd been to Florida. We'd seen what was happening. We were the first hotel in the area to have air conditioning. We had the first swimming pool in the area. Every nickel we could put our hands on went back into the resort. When I sold my airplane, we built the swimming pool.

Bullet's mother had some money in her estate that paid for the bar. I told Bullet at the time that his mother, who was a strong Christian, would be shocked if she knew he was using his inheritance to build a bar. I really didn't want a bar at Pine Needles, either. I came from a family of teetotalers — in fact, we didn't eat in restaurants that served liquor. Bullet and I didn't drink. But Bullet said, "We can't be in this business without a bar."

All the while our family was growing and allowing Bullet to fulfill a dream. When he worked for Spalding in Chicago in the late 1940s, he often visited a family-owned golf club where one brother was the pro, another the greenskeeper, another the cook. The sisters were waitresses in the dining room. He mentioned that place often — how he wanted to find a business his family could run together. He was getting his wish.

Bonnie was born in 1954, followed by Peggy Ann in 1958 and Kirk in 1962. We put the kids to work. They stuffed envelopes and hand-addressed them for a dime a day. Later they were counselors in our golf camps and instructors in our golf schools. In the summers, the resort slowed down, and Bullet, who loved to lie in the sun during lunch hour, would take the reservation charts to the pool, where he'd field inquiries for the coming season.

It was a challenge for both of us to juggle all our responsibilities around the resort and our home. I never really learned to cook, since as a girl I was interested in sports and later traveled so much playing golf. I told Bullet before we were married, "I can't cook."

He said that was okay: "Don't worry about it."

I learned that a pot roast was the perfect meal for me. Around lunch time, I could put a roast and some vegetables in the oven and leave it and go play golf. When I finished and came home, dinner would be ready. After Bonnie was born I had full-time live-in help that could cook, so we ate well.

Our guests and employees have given us a lot of pleasure over the years. We've had a lot of big names come through — Bing Crosby, Arnold Palmer, Jack Nicklaus, Pete and Alice Dye, George and Babe Zaharias, Patty Berg, Kathy Whitworth, Betsy King, Louise Suggs, Larry Nelson, Craig Stadler, Paul Azinger, Herb Wind, Bob Davies, Bob Scott, Dean Smith, Tom Landry, Jim Valvano, Mack Brown, Paul Anderson, Jimmy Carter, Sen. Terry Sanford, Perry Como, Gen. George Marshall, Sandra Day O'Connor, Gen. Omar Bradley, Bob Cousy, Ivan Lendl, James Garner, Michael Jordan, Dickie Smothers, Rudy Vallee and dozens more names you'd instantly recognize. Once Gen. Norman Schwarzkopf visited incognito. He was with a group and registered under another name, but he was easy to recognize.

We've also had a lot of loyal employees who have treated our guests like their guests. Martha in the kitchen and Virginia in the dining room have been with us for over 30 years. One of the best was Harold Williams, who actually pre-dated Bullet and me at Pine Needles. He was a lockerroom attendant when Bullet and I came in 1953 and later performed almost every task imaginable around the resort — painter, bartender, shop attendant. Harold had been a caddie as a young man and could hit the golf ball a mile. Bullet would show him off by taking him to the tee of the old first hole (now the eighteenth), and having him hit four-hundred yard drives to the green. In his later years, Harold provided our guests with the perfect shoeshine. When he died in 1995, we lost a little of the heart and soul of the resort.

Many golf writers, including Herbert Warren Wind, the late Bob Drum, the late Charlie Price and the late Dick Taylor, were tremendous help to us over the years. We've always had a great relationship with the press, and they've done a great job over the years in telling our story and spreading the word about what a special place Pine Needles (and now Mid Pines) has been.

In the final analysis, Pine Needles was successful because of Bullet. He was the glue that held the place together when I was out on the road, playing tournament golf. He was friendly with the guests, paternal but strict with the staff. He worked eighteen-hour days. He was always thinking ahead.

Bullet's father died when he was young, and he and his brother Russell grew up in modest surroundings. He never took anything for granted; part of the motivation for working long hours was that he wanted better for his children. He was also quick to help others who needed a break. Hundreds of young amateurs stayed at Pine Needles over the years at no charge while playing in local tournaments, including the North and South Amateur, and dozens of struggling young pros stayed here when the PGA Tour was making its regular stops at Pinehurst No. 2 in the 1970s. One of those was Pat McGowan, a nice young man from California who met Bonnie while staying at Pine Needles during the 1977 PGA Tour Qualifying School. They were married in November, 1981.

Bullet was never adverse to any job. He'd help cook breakfast if needed, then tee golfers off the first tee, then help make beds when the maids couldn't get in or were sick. He always helped to clean late into the night to save money.

He was an immaculate dresser. He wore ultra-suede jackets (when they were in style), his shirt sleeves were monogrammed, and the cuffs of his trousers had to fall one-half inch from front to back. The kids remember the famous occasion of Bullet getting his ultra-suede slacks and jacket covered in grease and mud while driving a moped during a vacation to Bermuda.

Bullet's blood pressure tended to be high, and he had his first real heart problem in 1965. He felt chest pains walking from the club to our house, which was along the eighteenth fairway. He went to the hospital the next day and was advised to rest for three weeks. Bullet was back at work in eight days and had another heart attack two weeks later.

Six years later, he had open-heart surgery. It was one of the first operations conducted where artery tissue from one part of the body was used to create a bypass into the heart (before that, they used plastic for the bypass). The doctors and hospital staff marveled at Bullet's ability to recover. He came home in a week and was quickly back to sixteen-hour days. The kids and I stayed on him about overload, and he eventually cut back to a more manageable schedule.

Bullet loved running his own business and being in charge. He once said he didn't want to be in business with anyone else, not even his own mother. No challenge was too large for him. Richard Tufts of Pinehurst told us late in 1970 that his brothers and other stockholders wanted to sell the resort and country club. If Malcolm McLean didn't buy it by Jan. 1, we could have it for $12 million. Bullet talked to a lot of people — banks, friends, family — about the idea of buying Pinehurst. He put the money together, but, unfortunately for us, McLean closed on the deal on Dec. 31. If we had gotten Pinehurst, Bullet would have figured out a way to run it.

Bullet was diagnosed with stomach cancer early in 1984 and died that May. Weeks before he died, he made the last payment on Pine Needles. He was proud that he could turn the resort over to his kids and their families, that Pine Needles could remain an informal and comfortable place for people to come play the grandest game on earth. Bullet talked a lot in later years about selling Pine Needles, and selling never crossed our minds after he died. There's too much sentimental value here. He built the place.

Thirty years ago, it was Bonnie, Peggy Ann and Kirk running around the place. Today it's their children — Blair, Melody, Kellyann, Grace, Michael and Scotti. I hope in thirty more years it'll be *their* children. I hope it will always stay that way.

CHAPTER 7
The Needles Of The Nineties

I can't believe that in 2001 we'll have our second U.S. Women's Open at Pine Needles. Little old Pine Needles, the course that looked so terrible in 1953 when Bullet and I and our partners bought it. No matter how bad it looked back then, it was still a Donald Ross gem and just needed some attention, some money and some nurturing back to health. It's exciting that it's getting the national recognition today that it deserves.

Pine Needles actually has been the site of several significant events in the evolution of women's golf.

The first competition ever held on the course was the inaugural Women's Mid-South Open Championship. Held in February, 1928, just after the course opened, the tournament was the first "open" golf competition for women in American history, according to *The New York Times*. "The time is ripe for such an event," the organizers said, noting that many top lady golfers were now professionals.

Bullet and I had the opportunity to have big-time golf at Pine Needles in the late 1960s. Joe Dey, executive director of the United States Golf Association, wrote in 1967 asking if we'd like to have the U.S. Women's Open at Pine Needles in 1969. All we had to do was put up a $20,000 purse.

Bullet and I wanted to do it, but we didn't think we could afford it. At the time, we were in debt building Pine Needles, so we didn't pursue it.

One tournament we did pursue was the Titleholders. Its board of directors decided in 1966 that it would temporarily suspend the tournament, which had been played in Augusta, Georgia, since 1937, while it researched the feasibility of continuing it at a later date. The Titleholders had a special place in our hearts because my winning there in 1949 was one of my biggest achievements in golf. It was like winning the Masters of women's golf. Bullet and I stayed with Mrs. Dorothy Manice, the tournament founder, many times in Augusta. We hated to see the tournament die. So we approached the board and said we'd do anything we could to resurrect it. In May, 1971, they in essence "gave us" the tournament, saying we had the rights and privileges of running it how and where and when we wanted.

So we moved the tournament to Pine Needles, and it was held in late May, 1972. We took a bath financially, but still it was fun having the tournament. Sandra Palmer won first place and a check for three grand as well as a green jacket and a small crown replicated after the original Titleholders trophy.

The large crown mounted and hanging over the wishing well in front of the Pine Needles clubhouse entrance today was a part of that Titleholders story. The Titleholders' identifying symbol was a crown, and Bullet had a forty-inch crown made of bronze as a permanent salute to the tournament. He also had smaller eight-inch crowns made to present to the champion and former champions. The price tag on all that hardware was more than Sandra won, to give you an idea of what prize money was like thirty years ago.

The tournament might have survived for years if the Augusta Titleholders committee had yielded to the idea of using a sponsor in the name of the tournament. At the time, however, title sponsorship wasn't as commonplace as it is today, and the tournament was dropped because of lack of a sponsor and other means of financial support. (The Titleholders was later resurrected by Sprint and then Mercury and played on the LPGA schedule from 1996-99).

And then the USGA came to Pine Needles in 1989 and 1991 with the Girls Junior Championship (won by Brandie Burton) and the Women's Senior Amateur (won by Phyllis Preuss). Having the latter championship at Pine Needles led to us getting the 1996 Women's Open. Serving on various USGA committees at the time were two long-time friends — Judy Bell (no relation), the first woman president of the USGA, and Barbara McIntire. Barbara had actually grown up in Toledo, Ohio, where we were friendly competitors. She later worked across the street at Mid Pines as a young lady and was a six-time winner of the Women's North and South Amateur at Pinehurst. She was also a two-time U.S. Women's Amateur champion and a British Women's Amateur champion. Barbara also received the 1999 USGA Bob Jones Award, the highest award in golf, which I received in 1990.

I was asked to welcome the senior ladies at the opening-night dinner. I said, "Well, we've had the USGA Junior and the USGA Senior. Now if we could get the U.S. Open, we'd have it covered."

Judy approached me afterward and said, "Would you like to have an Open here?"

I asked, "Are you kidding? Of course."

Judy said, "We'll work on it."

Later that fall, during the week in late October when the PGA Tour held its Tour Championship at Pinehurst No. 2, the USGA announced we would host the 1996 Women's Open at Pine Needles. What an incredible thrill! I joked that I probably wouldn't live long enough to see it. Of course I did, and it was an incredible week of perfect weather, huge crowds and great golf.

I was walking on a cloud, it seemed, the whole week. Several times, I looked up to the skies and said, "Thanks, Bullet. Great weather." Patty Berg, Louise Suggs and Kathy Whitworth came, and we gave a clinic early in the week. The purse was $1.2 million, with $212,500 to the winner. The purse for the 2001 Women's Open is $2.9 million. That's money the four of us can't comprehend for playing golf. We were amazed at the lifestyle these girls have on tour today. They have baby sitters and free meals and courtesy cars. I brought my baby sitter with me! Judy Rankin said not long ago that if she'd had the fitness trailer like they have today when she played, her career would have lasted a lot longer. Judy's back problems forced her off the tour, problems that stretching and exercise would have helped.

The only real question the USGA had was, "Would the people show up?" Southern Pines and Pinehurst are thought of as sleepy, out-the-way places, but actually they're within a hundred miles of seven million people — and a lot of them love golf. So the crowds were great, better than any of us anticipated. A record 110,000 golf fans attended.

What really pleased me about the week was how we had the ideal infrastructure to handle all the people — the golfers, officials, sponsors, media and spectators — particularly when you consider what Bullet and I started with almost fifty years ago. Corporate support within North Carolina was terrific. We never would have been successful with the 1996 or 2001 U.S. Women's Open without the Woman's Steering Committee, made up of top N.C. women executives. The State of North Carolina, the hundreds of volunteers, and Pinehurst Championship Management all played important roles in making our Championship so successful.

We had thought in the late-1980s and early-1990s about building a second golf course. We own some land to the north of the existing course — land that was used for parking during the Women's Open — and Pete Dye did a routing. We were getting close to pushing the button. But there was a glut of golf real estate and the economy turned sour during the Gulf War of 1990, so we tabled the plans for the time being. Then in 1994, we learned that Mid Pines was for sale. After more than twenty years of ownership, Manor Care Inc., of Silver Spring, Md., wanted to get out of the resort business. We talked to some potential investors and put together a group to buy Mid Pines. Having the inn and the golf course were perfect two years later during the Women's Open, as a lot of sponsors stayed there and played golf.

Mid Pines has been a wonderful addition to Pine Needles. I have so many great memories of the Cosgrove family, especially my dear friend Jean

Cosgrove Stevenson, who still works at Mid Pines, and playing that Donald Ross golf course. I tell people the real reason we bought Mid Pines was to get Chip King. Chip was the longtime head professional at Mid Pines, and when we bought the club, Chip became the director of golf for both courses. He's done a terrific job and is an outstanding golf professional. He's served as president of the Carolinas PGA and has won almost every award given by the PGA.

In the five years leading up to the Women's Open, we improved our facilities across the board at Pine Needles. We built the Golf Learning Center. We built a new cart-storage building and completely renovated our golf shop and men's and ladies' locker rooms. We renovated most of the rooms in the lodges. We rebuilt the range and sculpted target greens into the hitting area. The fairways were reseeded with 419 bermuda and all the greens were resprigged with bent. Across Ridge Road from the resort, we built a 14,500 square-foot building that housed media for the Open and is now a reception and meeting center. In the spring of 2001, we opened our four-hole, par-three course beside the Learning Center.

I was so proud of the way the family handled the week, and I know Bullet would have been proud as well. Having such a great Open was because of the groundwork Bullet laid so many years ago. Bullet would be proud of the way our son-in-law, Kelly Miller, has led the resort and the staff since the mid-1980s. Kelly is general manager of both resorts as well as general chairman of the 1996 and 2001 Women's Opens.

The only real scare we had was leading up to the Open. We had a heat wave in North Carolina about ten days before the championship started, and it threatened to burn out the thick, ryegrass rough that our course superintendent, Dave Fruchte, had worked so hard to cultivate. But Dave and his staff and a bunch of college kids went out on the golf course all day and hand-watered the roughs to keep the grass from dying. We were sweating it for a while, but then it cooled off the week of the Open and the course was perfect.

I already had the great fortune of developing a friendship with Annika Sorenstam, so the fact that she won the championship at Pine Needles made the week extra special. Annika went to college at the University of Arizona in the early 1990s, and there she made the acquaintance of my good friend and former U.S. Senior Women's Amateur champion, Edean Ihlanfeldt. One year Edean called to ask if this young Swedish girl could stay with me while playing in the Women's North and South at Pinehurst. So I got to know her that year and was tickled in 1995 when Annika won the Open at the Broadmoor. We hugged after the victory and I told her, "Now you can win it again at Pine Needles!" And she did!

One thing really stands out in my memory about Annika's performance that week. She played near-perfect golf, scoring rounds of 70-67-69-66 for a 272 total, six shots ahead of Kris Tschetter, but her one unfortunate break didn't disrupt her concentration or wreck her nerves. I happened to be standing behind the fourteenth green on Saturday, when Annika came through holding a two-stroke lead over Brandie Burton. Her four-iron approach rolled through the green and into heavy grass behind it. A photographer inadvertently stepped on her ball. She chipped on and three-putted, allowing Brandie to tie her. But Annika never blinked. She played the difficult finishing holes one-under, while Brandie stumbled back with two bogeys.

I asked her about the fourteenth hole later and she said, "I hit a great shot to the green — it just ran over. I would hit the same shot again." That's a great lesson for all golfers — focus on the positive, not the negative. The 59 that she shot in the LPGA Tournament in Phoenix in March of 2001, is more proof of her great golf.

The week was going so well that we talked on Friday night about asking the USGA to bring the Women's Open back to Pine Needles. We extended an invitation Saturday morning, not thinking anything would come of it until later. But Judy Bell, president of the USGA at the time, announced at the awards ceremony after the final round that we would get it back in 2001. Later I saw a picture of the family and all of us were just standing there with our mouths open and tears in our eyes. Judy said Pine Needles was the "Shinnecock of women's golf." That was quite a compliment.

CHAPTER 8
My Life and My Faith

Many years ago Bullet and I were visiting Hound Ears Resort up in the mountains of Western North Carolina, and Hugh Morton invited us over to his Grandfather Mountain attraction in Linville. Hugh asked if I wanted to hit some golf balls from the little golf tee he had at the top of the mountain, near the Mile High Swinging Bridge. The Rev. Billy Graham was to be there as well. I was honored and thrilled to meet him and be with him. He said he'd played golf that day, and I asked how he'd played. "I shot an eighty-two," he said. "If I'd played any better, I'd have to give up the ministry."

I'm glad Dr. Graham never got good enough to give up the ministry, and I thank the Lord for the wonderful message that he gives to the world. Billy's daughter, Ann Graham Lotz, and her husband, Dr. Danny Lotz, from Raleigh are good friends. Every January they bring the Fellowship of Christian Athletes retreat to Pine Needles with the two great speakers, Stewart and Jill Briscoe. This is the highlight of the year for me.

Not long ago a man named Tim Philpot directed a conference at Pine Needles titled "The Mulligan — Golf Lessons for Life." Tim was a collegiate golfer at the University of Kentucky, then a trial lawyer and later a Kentucky state senator. Today his organization, CBMC International, spreads the word of Christ and draws a number of parallels between golf and religion.

I was fascinated by his message. One of the most important to everyday living comes from Proverbs 16:9, where it says, "The human mind plans the way, but the Lord directs the steps." That tells us we can make certain plans and preparations, but in the end the will of God wins out.

It's the same in golf. We can prepare for a big tournament or a round of golf. We can "play the round" on the practice tee beforehand, imagining a certain tee ball and then a certain approach shot. We can practice the run-up putts we might have on a Donald Ross-designed course. We can visualize successful results before each shot.

But in the end, a sudden gust of wind, a wayward bounce on a sprinkler head, an unrelated thought that sneaks into our head at the worst second, can ruin all the preparation.

In those instances, we have to accept the things we have no control over, that bad breaks are a part of the game, that maybe we're dealt those breaks to learn how to overcome them. It's in overcoming what we cannot control that we build true character.

Byron Nelson is one of the great examples of how a strong spiritual life can help in golf and every facet of living. I've heard Byron talk about what a great life he's had, how many friends he's blessed with, the two terrific wives he's had — and all, he believes, because he's tried to do what the Bible has told him to do.

One of the best things about golf is that it reveals a person's character. The man or woman who cheats on the golf course will surely cheat in life.

In some six decades of playing golf, I'm amazed at how the game mirrors a good Christian life. Maybe that's why God led me to golf. With my upbringing and values, it was the perfect game for me. Teaching is fun because you feel like you are helping someone even if it is just a game.

I was so blessed that a strong spiritual life was handed down to me through both sides of my family. My paternal grandfather at the age of twenty was given a Bible before he came to America from his home in Scotland. Whenever he had a problem or was confronted with a difficult decision, he turned to Proverbs to find an answer. He was very successful in business and helped build a Presbyterian Church two doors down from the family home. My maternal grandfather was a Presbyterian minister. The church has always been a big part of my family's life.

I was taught as a child that America was founded on religion. Many of our ancestors came here to have the freedom to worship as they pleased. It was a vital part of our fabric in the beginning and still is, and should always be. I've seen Patty Berg give hundreds of clinics over the years. She always has small American flags along both sides of the clinic area, and in every one she concludes by saying, "God bless you, and God bless America."

Bullet went to church as a child, but unfortunately the preacher at his church just yelled to the congregation about everyone being sinners. That turned him off on going to church. But he nonetheless believed in God and lived a Christian lifestyle.

The perfect conduit for Bullet and me to bring our spiritual lives together was the Fellowship of Christian Athletes. That group has been immensely important in the lives of the Bell family and Pine Needles. Bullet absolutely loved having FCA groups at Pine Needles because they taught a wonderful message but did so in an informal, non-judgmental and non-preachy style. FCA is a wonderful group — coaches and athletes who believe in God. They are trying to direct the young men and women in this country to the Christian life and to get involved in their own churches. I'm proud to say that my daughter Bonnie started the first FCA for girls in the country at Pinecrest High School.

Captain Bill Lewis joined the FCA staff after his retirement from the Navy in 1968 and, living in the Washington area, organized a Bible study for the Baltimore Colts football team and gave the pre-game invocation at Washington Redskins' games. He began having devotions for players on the LPGA Tour in 1974 and soon after approached John Erickson, the president at the time of FCA, about starting a golf ministry. John told him there was no funding available at the time, but Bill had the green light if he wanted to start a program. The FCA golf ministry would become one of FCA's most strategic weapons in sharing the Christian faith. One of Bill's favorite messages was, "We all need the Jesus grip." When we are in Jesus's grip, Bill would say, we have His infinite love and power at our fingertips.

The FCA had its first national golf camp at Pine Needles in 1979. We've had all kinds of outstanding golfers active in FCA speak and teach at camp over the years. Larry Nelson, Wally Armstrong, Scott Simpson, Kenny Knox, Betsy King, Jerry Pate, Morris Hatalsky, Patty Berg and Alice Miller are just some of the golfers who have presented clinics, taught golf and stressed to these young people how you can't get by in life alone. You need God in your corner, you need to trust that the Lord will help guide your life to its fullest. Jack and Barbara Nicklaus sponsor the FCA International Pro-Am every fall at Loxahatchee Country Club in Jupiter, Fla.; they've raised more than $2.5 million since 1985 for the FCA golf ministry. This money is why FCA is able to have eighteen junior golf camps across the country each year.

Our FCA camps have been so much fun and so rewarding over the years that often we've asked, "Why can't we offer this same experience for adults?" Toward that goal, in September of 2001 we're hosting the inaugural FCA Adult Golf Dream Weekend. We'll have one hundred and twenty golfers in for a weekend of golf instruction, competition, entertainment and great Christian fellowship.

I was on the FCA Board of Directors for six years, and that was a great experience. It was a big thrill for me to sit on the board and see people like Tom Landry, the coach of the Dallas Cowboys, and Lamar Hunt, the owner of the Kansas City Chiefs, and how much God and the use of prayer influenced and affected their lives. Tom became a good friend. I was so sad to see him leave the Cowboys and then succumb to leukemia in February, 2000. I've never known a man more dedicated to the Lord than Tom Landry. In his autobiography, Coach Landry summarized his life philosophy: "If your priority is football, then you're going to suffer a whole lot. You have very little control over a whole lot of things. When your priority is God first and your family second, then everything falls into place."

I'm not sure how we would have survived the early days of running Pine Needles without a strong faith in God. Bullet and I were literally winging it. We knew golf, but we didn't know the hotel business. We had a little money, but certainly not enough to expand the facilities the way we needed to when we lost the lease on the original pro shop, dining room and sleeping quarters. We just put our faith in God that in the end, it would work out, for better or worse. If God had directed us back to Findlay to take over my dad's wholesale grocery business, He would never have led us to the wonderful life that my family and I are enjoying today. To me it is all as simple as that.

Golf has taken me around the world, and it's been interesting to learn about the spiritual lives of other cultures. I went to India for two weeks in 1994 to coach the India women's golf team, and the young girls took me into several different temples, where they prayed. One girl said to me, "It doesn't matter what you pray to, as long as you know there's something out there greater than yourself."

I've known golfers who openly talk about their faith — Tom Lehman, Corey Pavin, Paul Azinger, Bernhard Langer, Larry Nelson, Scott Simpson, Larry Mize, Nancy Lopez and Betsy King among them.

Langer's won two Masters, and he's talked about the difference in winning in 1985 and 1993. He had found a relationship with Christ by the time the second victory came, and he noted in the television interview afterward how significant it was to have won it on Easter Sunday. "God replaced my reliance on winning and on things with the peace of God's love," he said.

When Betsy was inducted into the LPGA Hall of Fame, she contributed her Bible for display because she had studied it all the while on tour and it had provided daily guidance. Most people donate a ball or club they used to win a major championship; Betsy contributed her Bible. That was a special gesture from a special person. Betsy, incidentally, makes time every summer to attend at least one FCA golf camp.

I remember when Corey Pavin first came onto the PGA Tour. I didn't like watching him very much. Later, I noticed a difference in him. He'd changed. He seemed to smile more and enjoy himself more. I mentioned that to Pat McGowan one day, and Pat said, "Didn't you know? He's turn to Christianity." It was remarkable that I could tell a difference without even knowing him or knowing anything about his religious beliefs.

I can remember when Larry Nelson won the U.S. Open, in 1983 at Oakmont. He was scheduled to be at our FCA camp the following day. We would have understood if he'd cancelled. Bill Lewis called him and told him that. But Larry said no, he'd made a commitment. The kids were so excited and made a big banner to welcome him. He was there as scheduled and showed that such a big moment wasn't going to overshadow a commitment to serve the Lord.

Another good friend of ours at Pine Needles is Wally Armstrong, a former PGA Tour player who has written a book with Dr. Jim Sheard titled, *Finishing the Course — Strategies for the Back Nine of*

Your Life. It's an outstanding little book filled with ideas on improving your golf and your faith. Its theme is that it doesn't matter how you start in golf or in life — it's how you finish that counts.

It was a moving experience in 1999 to see Payne Stewart win the U.S. Open at Pinehurst after being led to the Lord over the last few years by his children. People all over the world wondered what that bracelet on his right wrist stood for — W.W.J.D. It meant "What would Jesus do?" and was given to him by his son. I wear one just like it. I'm so glad Payne found the Lord before God took him from us. I don't know why Payne was taken from our midst at the height of his career, but I have faith the answer will be revealed. I do feel that through his death, his Christian spirit has lived on and has had far-reaching effect.

I had a wonderful experience and one that I will always cherish after Payne won the Open. My granddaughter Melody wanted his autograph on a Pinehurst flag and asked me to get it for her. I waited for him until he came back into the clubhouse after all the press interviews and stopped him just before he was going on the air with Andy North on ESPN. He grabbed me, turned to a camera and said, "Get this picture." He looked at me and said, "The Lord really blessed me today." He signed the flag and moved on. That is a moment I will always remember.

Payne Stewart was given a mulligan in life, and he made the best of it. We all have that same opportunity as well.

CHAPTER 9
My Life As A Teacher

I had never given a golf lesson in my life when my husband, Bullet, came up to me one day in 1954. He pointed to a woman who had come into the Pine Needles golf shop and said, "That woman wants to learn to play golf. Go teach her."

At the time, our clientele was nearly a hundred percent men, and seeing a woman wanting to learn the game took Bullet by surprise.

"I don't know what to tell her," I said, trying to beg out of the job.

"You know more golf than she does," Bullet said. "Tell her anything."

So there I went. And it was a disaster. I hope I refunded the woman's $2 fee for the golf lesson.

I took her outside our golf shop. At the time, we were operating out of two buildings near the original Pine Needles Inn, today the St. Joseph's of the Pines extended-care facility behind the current eighteenth and second tees. One of those buildings no longer exists, but the one used as a pro shop and dining room still stands, tucked in the woods to the left of the first fairway (it's used now as offices for St. Joseph's). There was no real practice area, just a small area of turf outside the pro shop, where two or three golfers could hit shots across today's first fairway.

I told her everything I knew. We were out there for two or three hours. She'd hit it badly and I'd say, "Try this." Another bad shot. "Try this." I was going crazy trying to get her to hit it like I could.

Finally, she said, "Can we quit? I'm dead." I didn't blame her. But I would have stayed there until midnight. I often wonder about that poor woman. I'm sure she quit golf then and there.

That lesson sparked my interest in teaching. I soon developed a close relationship with Ellen Griffin of the Woman's College of the University of North Carolina (today UNC-Greensboro). Ellen was an early teaching professional and a pioneer in women's golf instruction. We were having lunch one day at Pine Needles in 1959 when Bullet bemoaned the fact that a business group, which had booked the entire resort for one week the following month, had just canceled.

"Bullet, let's put in a golf school for women," Ellen said.

"We can't do that. No one will come," Bullet said.

"Well, let's try," Ellen said with conviction.

So we took out an ad in *Golf World* magazine. We charged $105 for four days and three nights. We had video equipment, which was a brand new thing then. We sent out mimeographed flyers to all the country clubs in North Carolina. We had fifty-three women at that first school and were off and running in the golf school and instruction business. I don't know of anyone else in the country doing golf schools at that time. Winning the 1989 Ellen Griffin Rolex Award, the highest honor within the LPGA's Teaching & Club Professional Division, was really special to me. I am very proud of that award. Ellen was a big influence on my teaching career. She knew early on that there was a vacuum of women teaching women. The award is dedicated to Ellen's spirit, love and dedication to the golf student, teaching skills and game of golf.

Since then, thousands of women golfers have learned more about the game at Pine Needles. So have men (we started men's golf schools in 1988, which have evolved into our Learning Center Schools for men and women). Couples, families and youngsters have learned the game as well through an assortment of family and youth camps and through the annual Fellowship of Christian Athletes golf camp.

From the beginning Ellen came up with the word "Golfari" for our women's golf schools. It's a take-off on the word "safari" and means a "week-long excursion into golf." A full house of ladies, usually around 140, arrive on Sunday afternoon during Golfari weeks in February, May and September. Each day begins with a clinic with me and my son-in-law, former PGA Tour pro Pat McGowan, followed by instruction, lunch and then golf in the afternoon. Following dinner, there's usually a lecture or clinic or instruction video. It's "gal's week out" with golf being the common thread.

Golfaris are great fun for me, but the great staff and Pat are the real reasons the schools are so popular. Pat has a great personality and makes learning fun for all students. You almost have to come to Pine Needles to understand what I'm saying. He's one of the main reasons we've been so successful. My daughter Bonnie is also a great help to me and loves the game as much as I do. She is an excellent teacher. In fact, I have turned most of my private lessons over to her. I know she is a much better teacher than I am.

I admit I didn't know a lot about what I was doing in the early days. Besides Ellen, the person I give a lot of credit to for helping me in the beginning was Lee Kosten, a long-time teaching pro whom I befriended while playing golf in Florida in the early 1950s. We offered Lee a teaching job at Pine Needles in 1958.

Lee told me that everything starts with the grip, and to this day I'm a stickler for getting the grip correct. Then he helped me with the takeaway and other parts of the swing. Why I felt so inadequate in teaching was that I'd never thought about anyone's game but my own. I think what everybody does is teach how they play. I had to have more than that. A lot of women would come to Pine Needles to take a lesson from a woman pro. Lee would always help me with them. I didn't feel qualified without him in the early days. When I'd get stuck with a lesson, I'd turn to Lee. We always taught side-by-side in the schools. I wanted him right by me.

At first, I was nervous teaching men but later relaxed as I saw the result of emphasizing that power comes from a well-timed swing instead of hands and elbows flying and flailing and wrists snapping.

I learned early in my teaching career that in addition to the grip, it's vitally important to get stance, posture, ball position and alignment correct. How you swing is a function of how you set up. Most bad swings begin with something being wrong from a static position or set up.

All teachers eventually learn how important the mental aspect of the swing is in learning. One thing I know is that the mind controls the body. Until you understand your golf swing, you will never reach your potential.

Pine Needles was the site every summer from the mid-1970s through the late-1980s of National Golf Foundation summer teaching seminars. At the time, education and instruction were important components of the NGF's program of work, and it held annual seminars at several sites around the country to show health and physical education instructors in public high schools how to teach golf and start golf programs in their schools. Staff instructors and guest speakers such as Conrad Rehling, DeDe Owens, Ellen Griffin, Jim Flick, Gary Wiren, Peter Kostis, Bob Rotella, Rod Myers, Dick Gordin, Bob Toski, Carol Johnson, Jim Suttie, Wally Armstrong, Bill Strausbaugh, Shirley Spork, Ann Casey Johnstone and others attended over the years, imparting their wisdom to the physical education teachers to take back home and spread among the masses.

The LPGA took a major step in 1959 by creating the Teaching & Club Professional Division, which is committed to advancing the sport through teaching, managing golf facilities and coaching rising stars. One of my greatest honors was being named to the T&CP Hall of Fame when it was inaugurated in 2000 along with Marilynn Smith, Petty Berg, Shirley Spork, Betty Hicks and Louise Suggs. I thought it was very fitting that the 2000 T&CP Championship was held at Mid Pines Inn & Golf Club, the resort we added to our family in 1994.

I picked up a lot of images and swing mechanics watching and learning from other great players over the years, and I began to use those to found the bedrock of my teaching fundamentals.

Byron Nelson had taken over as pro at Inverness Country Club in Toledo in 1940, and I distinctly remember his hip and lower-body motion. I tried to copy it. He had kind of a rocking motion, with both legs very flexible as they moved into and through the ball. Tommy Armour taught me to hit down on the ball, which was a great thought for ladies because they try so hard to scoop the ball up. Watching Sam Snead ingrained the need to make a full shoulder turn. I remember the plane of Ben Hogan's swing more than anything. One year in the late 1940s the LPGA Tour was in Fort Worth, and I went to Colonial Country Club to watch him practice. I watched him for two hours and the caddie shagging balls barely moved. After he finished practicing, we walked back to the clubhouse and he talked about changing his swing to fade the ball. He said his hook was costing him too many tournaments.

At one point in the late 1950s, Bullet decided to dig up the swampy area where the driving range now sits and make it a lake.

"You'll be able to sit up in the dining room and look out over the lake," he said.

I had my eye on that area for a practice range.

"But where will I practice?" I asked.

I told him that if we had a practice range there, people could hit balls while waiting to tee off. He agreed not to build the lake. Then he decided that if we were going to have a practice range, it had better be a good one. He built the practice shelters and installed mats so that instruction could continue and guests could practice in bad weather. He built my private teaching center up to the left of the range and a large teaching tee up on the hill to the right. On the opposite end of the range, there is room for 40 students to hit balls.

After Dr. Jim Suttie came to Pine Needles and started our Golf Learning Center, we took another major step in 1992 with the construction of our Golf Learning Center building. Jim was with us for several years in the early 1990s and is one of the top teachers in the country (he was the PGA 2000 Teacher of the Year). Our 4,000-square foot building at the far end of the practice range has a two-bay indoor video station, seven sheltered practice stations, classroom space and an indoor putting area. It's loaded with gadgets and teaching aids to help with everything from keeping elbows from flying to learning to hit off sidehill and downhill lies. There's no doubt that the best gadget of the last twenty years is the development of video equipment. It's unbelievable how helpful video is in teaching. Seeing is believing. When a player sees himself on tape, he understands what the problem is.

Our Beginners Golfaris are one of our latest innovations. Entering the world of golf can be a daunting proposition for a lot of people, particularly women. Not only do you have to learn to hit the ball, but you have to learn the "lingo" of the game, how to keep score, how the rules work, where to drive the cart and where *not* to drive it, course etiquette and so many other things that seasoned golfers take for granted. Our Beginners Golfaris focus on those issues along with the basic fundamentals of the golf swing.

The bottom line in teaching is that you really care about your student learning to play the game. Sometimes you can be struggling, struggling, struggling with a student, and then all of a sudden the light comes on and he gets it. Watching him hit the ball flush and seeing the smile on his face makes it all worthwhile.

There is not one week that goes by that I don't get a letter or phone call from someone who's been in a Golfari and has a success story. They've broken a hundred. They've broken ninety. They've won the club championship.

In February, 2001, a lady named Evelyn Tucci from Beachwood, Ohio called from Florida where she and her husband spend the winter, to tell me she'd made two holes-in-one in one round of golf — they even came within the same nine holes! That in itself is unbelievable. What makes the story more exciting is that Evelyn is eighty-two years old! She was playing at Crystal Lake Country Club in Pompano Beach and was featured on *Good Morning America* after her accomplishment. Florida Governor Jeb Bush even called to congratulate her and set up a golf date with her. We've got another woman, Virginia White of Pleasanton, California, who's in her nineties now and has been coming to a Golfari for thirty-three years. She still loves to play. We bend the rules a little and let her ride right up to the green.

These stories are what really make you glow.

In the next chapter, I offer a few of my teaching and golf philosophies and some anecdotes from six decades of playing, competing, teaching and just generally "hanging around" the game of golf.

Chapter 10
My Tips for Better Golf

Golf Begins With The Grip

One of the first things we do when a golfer comes to Pine Needles for a Golfari (our eight-times-a-year women's schools) or a Golf Learning Center (smaller schools held throughout the year) is give him or her a "reminder form grip."

I am absolutely sold on the benefits of a proper grip. It is so important to a proper swing! We buy these training aids by the box full that are made of rubber and are formed so that, when you grip one, you are assuming the almost perfect golf grip.

With this aid, you can't grip it wrong. If a student has a poor grip, that's where we start. We even have some golf clubs with the grip guides mounted on them; students hit balls with the correct grips until the grip begins to feel natural.

First of all you have to have fun at our schools. When you look at my hands I have painted the last three fingernails on my glove hand in red and the middle two fingernails on my opposite hand. Then I tell them the nails painted in red are the grippers and the unpainted fingers are the feelers.

One key thing to remember with the grip is that you do not hold the club with the meat, or the palm, of the hand. The grip of the club should be enveloped more where the palm meets the fingers. I have a little trick where I use a black permanent

102

marker on a white golf glove to help people grip the club correctly. I bet I do that for ninety percent of our Golfari students. Sometimes a golfer will come back the next year and say, "Will you mark up two gloves for me? I'd like to have an extra to take home."

Grip pressure is an important issue as well. Babe Zaharias used to say, "I grip it soft at the start because I know it will tighten on the way down." She knew it was a natural move to increase your grip pressure as you make the turn down and into the ball. If she started from a tight pressure position, going tighter would reduce her flexibility and feel. Ben Hogan always said that he tried to maintain the same grip pressure throughout the swing.

Two subtle parts of the grip I think are crucial — a "short thumb" with the left hand (assuming you're a right-handed golfer) and a "trigger finger" with the right forefinger.

When the left thumb is positioned on the top of the grip, just a little right of center, you'll find you have several options with the actual placement. You can stretch the thumb as far down the grip as it will go, or you can pull it up, so that it's close to the left forefinger.

When I first started playing golf, my thumb was stretched so far down the grip, in a "long" position, that it actually stood out from underneath the thumb of my right hand. My first golf teacher, Leonard Schmutte, the pro at Findlay Country Club in Ohio, looked at it and said, "Your thumb's too long."

"But I'm hitting it great!" I told him.

"You won't for long," he responded.

Since then I've preferred the shorter position because I think it tends to support the last three fingers of the left hand better. If you have a long thumb, you can have too much wrist cock in the swing. There are exceptions to everything, though. Fred Couples uses a long thumb; it helps him cock his wrists and generate some of his incredible club-head speed.

The trigger finger — or the forefinger of the right hand, assuming you're a right-handed golfer — should always be positioned just below the thumb on the clubshaft. This will improve your feel throughout the swing and give you more control of the clubhead. The last three fingers of the left hand and the middle two fingers of the right hand are the grippers, and the forefingers are the feelers.

Placing the hands on the golf club is indeed an art. I prefer a smaller, thinner grip on my clubs. Tommy Armour always had the smallest grip possible put on his clubs. He believed you have more feel with a thinner grip. If the grip is fat, you tend to grab it like a baseball bat and want to wale away at the ball. A thinner grip allows you to feel the clubhead more throughout the swing. Les Bolstead, the great teacher of Patty Berg, always said that in selecting golf clubs, the grip size was as important as getting the proper shaft length and weight of the club. His theory was that if you had small hands, get small grips; medium hands, get medium grips; large hands, get large grips.

One last reason to have a great grip — it influences the all-important elbows. If your grip is sound and your posture is good, your elbows will tend to hang straight down from your shoulders, and your left arm and the clubshaft will make a straight line to the ball.

Be vigilant over your grip. Patty Berg always

said, "Check your grip daily because it has a tendency to change."

So if you take anything from this book, take this — Get A Grip!

Spot Every Shot

Aiming every shot in golf, from a three-foot putt to a drive, is much easier with the age-old practice of "spotting" the ball. This is an important technique for all beginners to ingrain into their games. In lining up a putt, stand behind the ball and pick a spot on your target line five to eight inches in front of the ball. Then set the blade of the putter so your ball will roll over that spot. Do the same thing with chips and pitches. With full shots, you might pick a spot about three feet in front of your ball. Make sure your clubface is lined up with your spot. Essentially you've brought your target much closer, allowing your aim to improve dramatically.

Think Box, Go Box

Most golfers are guilty of standing over a shot with too many thoughts racing through their minds. It's nearly impossible to hit a good shot with your head full of stuff. You stand there and freeze because all the clutter in your mind is keeping you from pulling the trigger.

A good mental trick is the "Think Box, Go Box."

Standing behind the ball, you're in the "Think Box." Find your target. Check the wind. Review your swing thoughts and fundamentals taking a practice swing and visualize the shot your are about to hit.

Then stand up to the ball and check your alignment.

Now you're in the "Go Box." Visualize the shot and swing through to the finish. Hit the shot with nothing cluttering your mind.

The Little Circle Waggle

I used to spend a lot of time in the winter playing tournament golf, and between tournaments Babe Zaharias and I often visited Tommy Armour in Boca Raton. We'd have lessons in the morning and then tee it up with Tommy in the afternoon. Tommy's first lesson with me was to teach me to waggle. He showed me how to take the club straight back from the ball several inches, then circle back down inside the line, just as the swing itself should be. "It's the swing in miniature," he said. To this day I still use the little circle waggle.

A forward press is a good element to the waggle as well. It's a signal to the mind and body to "Start the swing. Go. Quit standing there!"

But no matter what kind of waggle you develop, it's important to keep some part moving to keep you relaxed as you stand over the ball. If you're completely still, you can lock up and never pull the trigger in the same sequence every swing. You might move your feet a little; you might move your head to take one last look at the target. It's like dancing. There's a rhythmic flow to everything.

Low And Slow It Goes

The takeaway of the full swing and the putt can benefit by using one of my favorite swing thoughts, "Low and slow."

Mickey Wright used to say that if she could take the driver back eight inches "low and slow," she'd hit a good drive. Often I'll place a golf ball on the ground, about eight inches behind the ball a player is addressing. I have the player push that ball on the backswing, moving it no more than eight or ten feet. That guarantees a low, slow takeaway. A lot of people want to snatch the club back with the right hand. That's a recipe for disaster.

I use the same thought on the putting green. I'll be over a putt and I'll think, "Low and slow." That prevents me from lifting the putter head and from jerking the stroke. Then I add one thought to it: "Accelerate through." That reminds me that I have to give the ball a "firm stroke" coming through it. If you decelerate when you hit a putt, you'll hit it off line and lose the solid roll the ball has to have on short putts. Don't wish it in.

Pinching The Knees

An overlooked part of the golf swing is the footwork. You wouldn't build a house on a weak foundation. Your feet and legs are the foundation of the golf swing, and if their movements aren't correct, your swing doesn't have much of a chance.

Tommy Armour used to talk about "pinching the knees," the act of putting your weight on the insides of each foot — and particularly the right foot — at address and throughout the swing. He used to take his golf shoes to a cobbler and have him insert four small screws in the inside edges of his shoes. He used those screws for added traction. He used to say, "Peggy, these are the spikes for swinging the club. The other spikes are for walking." This thought or drill is used when golfers sway.

A lot of golfers get far too much weight on the outsides of their feet, particularly the right foot, which doesn't allow them to shift back to their left side and let their head drift ahead of the ball before impact.

During a lesson I will often place a sandwedge face-down under the outside of the golfer's right foot. That helps him feel what it's like to have the weight on the inside of his foot.

The Left Heel

The movement of the left heel (or lack thereof) is another important element of footwork and is the source of spirited debate in the golf world.

Jack Nicklaus is the greatest golfer ever, and he lifted his left heel high off the ground during the backswing. Babe Zaharias wasn't too shabby a player either and was the longest hitter in my day. She lifted her left heel a good inch — then slapped it down to start her down swing.

The first time I played golf with Glenna Collett Vare, one of the first great ladies of golf, I noticed how quickly she lifted her left heel and then slapped it back down. "That's her secret," I said excitedly to myself, and started copying her.

Helen Sigel Wilson, who was playing with us, asked me, "What on earth are you doing?"

"I'm trying to copy Glenna's foot action," I said.

Helen responded: "That popping up and down is probably the worst part of Glenna's swing."

Glenna had a fast swing and great timing, and this foot action worked for her. But for most golfers, myself included, the left heel is best kept right where it is — on the ground. But don't let this thought keep you hanging on the left side. Your weight has got to be transferred to the right foot on the backswing. If the golfer is not flexible the left heel can come off on the back swing, but remember this the first move on the down swing is the lower body.

Keep The Post

Ninety percent of the golfers I've taught are afflicted with one major problem — they sway their hips to the right on the backswing (for a right-handed golfer).

The solution to this is to "keep the post" on the backswing. In other words, pivot around the flexed right leg. The right leg must feel as if it's staying in the same position, with almost the same knee flex, throughout the backswing. The weight should go on the inside of the right foot on the backswing. This turning the right hip "around the post" will provide a solid right side and will help you drive through the ball on the follow through. The lower body provides a lot of power and clubhead speed, so keeping that post secure is extremely important.

The Pause That Refreshes

There's no doubt that the change in directions at the top of the backswing is one of the toughest parts of the game. It's difficult to get all the parts moving in sync from the backswing to the downswing. Most golfers tend to rush it because they want to hit the ball.

A simple reflection on the laws of physics can give you an idea of the importance of a little pause at the top of the backswing. If an object is going in one direction and then is going to reverse itself and go in the opposite direction (as your hands and arms do in the golf swing), they *have* to come to a complete stop — even if it's just for a millisecond.

Some golfers can't feel that stop and that change of direction any more than they can see whether their clubface is open or shut at impact. But if you'll make an effort on the practice tee to pause at the top — I call it "the pause that refreshes" — it will slow your swing down, improve your tempo and improve your downward action.

It's also a good vantage for two important check points at the top of your backswing — your back should be to the target and your head should be behind the ball.

Turn and Return

One day in the early 1980s, Jack Nicklaus came to Pine Needles to do a clinic for Hart Shaffner & Marx, the clothing line he represented. As he was warming up on the practice tee, he took a club, put it across his back about waist high and wrapped his arms over it. Then he assumed a golf stance and posture and turned back behind the ball, then returned back through it. He was really just loosening up, but he demonstrated a very basic fundamental of body motion, one that I use frequently today.

The golf swing, in essence, is turning back, and turning through.

Turn, and return.

Turn, and return.

I've told that story often over the years and said, "If it's good enough for Jack Nicklaus, it's good enough for the rest of us."

Elbow In The Watch Pocket

Think of putting your right elbow into your "watch pocket," or right-hand pocket, on the downswing. That's an idea I've heard since I was a kid, which reminds me that there's not much new about

110

the golf swing. We have better equipment and balls. We have video and multitudes of new devices. We have great lies in the fairway and smooth putting surfaces. But the basics of the game haven't changed in a hundred years.

If you look at any athletic move involving the arms, the elbow always leads. Think of those old photos of Sandy Koufax throwing a fastball for the Dodgers. His elbow is way in front of his hand. A tennis player has to lead with the elbow on a serve or a groundstroke; otherwise, the motion will be wristy and weak.

Therefore, the left elbow leads as the right elbow drops on the way down in the golf swing. If not, you're releasing the club way too soon — and losing all your distance. So stick that right elbow in your watch pocket — and watch the ball fly.

Head Stays Back

One of Bob Jones' key fundamentals is that the head always stays behind the ball through impact. He always said, "I swing by my chin." Nancy Lopez says that's the No. 1 mistake she sees amateurs make — their head moves ahead of the ball.

Posing For Perfection

Tommy Armour was a stickler for "holding the finish" of the golf swing. He hammered that point home over and over as we worked on the practice range at Boca Raton over those many winters in the forties and fifties. "Hold the finish until the ball stops rolling," he'd say. Try that sometime and you'll see how difficult it is.

Once at the All-American at Tam O'Shanter in Chicago, Betsy Rawls, LPGA Hall of Famer, teed off on the first hole on the first day. The All-American was the first tournament to build spectator bleachers around greens and tees. There were more people around that first tee than we'd ever seen before, and understandably it made us more nervous than normal.

Betsy teed her ball, swung and cold topped it right into a creek that ran in front of the tee. But she held that finish. She posed and posed and looked as if she'd cracked one 250 yards instead of burying it in the drink.

That's amazing concentration and discipline — to hold that finish, no matter what.

To Tommy, holding the finish was a means to an end. He figured that if you finished facing the target and in balance, all the parts up until that point were working in the correct sequence. If you're lunging or just swinging the arms, the body will not finish toward the target. If you're coming across the ball, your arms will be wrapped around you instead of in that nice, high position. If you finish correctly, you should be able to recoil — turn back to your backswing in balance.

The Graceful Golf Swing

"Grip it and rip it" works for John Daly, but that's not the image that works well for most golfers.

Once I was giving a lesson to a couple of football players. They were big and muscular and lurched over the ball and gave it a whack for all it was worth. They felt like they could melt the ball with a powerful swing. I put a speed meter on them and they were swinging at fifty or sixty miles an hour and going nowhere. Then I'd swing the club, nice and smooth, and measure ninety-five miles an hour. They couldn't believe it. It went against every grain of macho man in their bodies that an old lady could generate more speed than these young, strapping boys. But they didn't understand what the golf swing should be. It's smooth, rhythmical, graceful, fluid. It's like the ballet. People need to visualize the golf swing smoothly back and accelerate smoothly through. It's not about gouging and grabbing and digging and lunging.

The All-Important Short Game

There was a girl on the LPGA Tour in the early days named Bonnie Randolph. She was a nice player, but she didn't hit the ball very far and was pretty far down the money list. We all went home in the fall, and when we came back out the next year, she won the first tournament.

Everyone was shocked. We asked her, "What have you been doing?"

She said she went home and did nothing but work on her short game for two months. She chipped, pitched, hit bunker shots and putted. The results were amazing.

That goes to show you what kind of difference you can make in your bottom-line scores with more attention to the short game.

If I go into a slump, sometimes I'll quit hitting balls and spend my practice time on the short game and taking practice swings. These short practice swings are valuable because they take your mind

113

off the ball and help you build fundamentally to the full swing.

Think Left To Chip Right

The majority of golfers I've taught over the years share one common fault: They're haunted by an assortment of fat and bladed shots from around the green that prevents them from getting "up and down" and turning bogeys into pars. Most of them benefit by emphasizing the left side in chipping. Address the ball with an open stance while keeping your shoulders parallel to the target line, with most of your weight on your left side, the ball centered or back and your hands slightly ahead of the ball. Then let the left hand and arm together control the stroke back and through the ball. By keeping the right hand quiet, you avoid trying to scoop the ball. The shoulders and arms work together as a pendulum stroke.

Two Clubs For The Short Game

If you're a beginner or an experienced player plagued by inconsistency around the green, let's simplify your short game.

Learn to play two clubs.

First, your seven-iron. When chipping, I know that the seven-iron will carry one-third the distance to the hole and roll the other two-thirds. In other words, if you have thirty feet to the flag and plenty of green to work with, hit the ball ten feet and watch it roll twenty more. Of course, you have to take into account the speed of the greens and any elevation changes.

Second, a wedge (a pitching wedge or sand wedge), for shots where the ball has to get up and

114

down quickly to traverse a bunker, a ridge or a mound in the green.

So instead of trying to master a handful of clubs around the greens, learn to play these two well to develop feel.

A law that golf should have when chipping: Putt when you can; Chip when you have to; Pitch when you have no other choice.

Long Lost Putter

The LPGA Tour was in Phoenix one year, some time in the early-1950s, when a man with curly hair approached me on the putting green.

"Peggy, would you give this new putter a try?" asked the man, who introduced himself as Karsten Solheim.

It seems that Solheim, an engineer with General Electric living in Phoenix, had become enthralled with improving the game's implements since taking up golf a few years earlier. In particular, he had an idea for a putter that he hoped could supplant the blade putter that was the most popular model of the day.

Solheim assembled the working model for his first putter, the 1-A, by laying two sugar cubes on a table five inches apart and gluing popsicle sticks between them. He drew the design for another putter, the one he was holding in his hand that day in Phoenix, on the back of a seventy-eight-rpm record sleeve. It was an odd-looking putter and was the first perimeter-weighted club I'd ever seen. It had a cavity back design for heel-toe balance and an off-set hosel.

I stroked a few balls with it and noticed more

than anything the distinctive sound it made when it struck the ball — that "ping" that would later be the name of Solheim's club manufacturing company. He told me he originally named the club the "Answer," but the six letters wouldn't fit on the club. So his wife suggested he remove the "W."

Thus the "Anser" putter. I didn't know I was holding a piece of golf history in my hands. That club would be the cornerstone to the club-making business Karsten built. Of course, later he expanded the perimeter-weighting concept to irons and revolutionized the equipment business. Karsten was also a great friend of women's golf, as he pioneered the Solheim Cup, the women's equivalent to the Ryder Cup, in 1990. It was a sad day when he died in February, 2000.

Karsten gave me that club and I used it for about three years, but in the end traded it to another pro for his putter. I wonder where that club is today.

The putter is without question the most personal golf club in the bag. People have love affairs with their putters. And they get divorces. Julius Boros once gave up on an old blade putter and switched to a different model. Later that putter was stolen, so he went back to the discarded blade. The old feeling came back, and he started winning.

Drop The Putts
The putting stroke is also the one move in the game that is subject to dozens of personal nuances. There's no one correct way to putt, but two constants found in the strokes of every good putter are that, one, the club accelerates through the ball, and, two, the head and body stay still throughout the motion and even after the putt is stroked. I often tell

my students to keep their head down until they hear the sound of the ball dropping into the cup.

I was playing with my longtime friends Pete and Alice Dye one day not long ago, and Alice was intent on keeping her head still.

She stroked one putt that, unfortunately, lipped out, and asked, "Did that miss on the left?" She was keeping her head down so long that she missed seeing what happened to the ball. That's a bit extreme, perhaps, but it reflects her effort to keep her head still and down. Alice made a fair number of putts that afternoon, by the way. She has always been a wonderful putter.

The putt on the seventy-second hole that Payne Stewart made to win the 1999 U.S. Open at Pinehurst was the result of concentrating on keeping his head still. His wife, Tracey, had pointed out to him Saturday night that several key putts he'd missed in the third round were because his head was moving. All he thought about on the eighteenth green was keeping his head still. He gave his wife credit for his victory.

Never Cozy The Short Ones

Most people try to play too much break on short putts. Sometimes they'll play them a ball or more outside the hole and "cozy" the ball toward the cup, hoping it will die in the hole.

I've taken the opposite approach as long as I've been playing golf. I'm very aggressive on short putts. I'll borrow a little, maybe right-center or left-center, but for the most part I keep the ball in the hole and stroke it firmly. You'll have much better results this way. Feel is a great thing with longer putts. For the short ones, bang 'em home.

The Eye Drop Test

Sometimes a golfer will feel like he's making a good stroke on the greens, but nothing will fall into the hole. Often this is a result of poor aiming, which is caused by poor head position at address.

Try this: Assume address position and hold a golf ball between your eyes. Now drop it. If your eyes are positioned directly above your ball on the green, the dropped ball will hit the one on the green. If it misses, adjust your head position until you get it right. The putts will start to fall.

Make Putting Fun

Practicing putting can be very boring if you don't enliven it with some sort of "game." Here are a couple of drills that will help on long putts and short putts.

Speed is the key on approach putts of twenty to thirty feet. Most three-putts result from leaving these putts way short or hitting them too hard. Take tees and string, or chalk or lime, and make a circle three feet in diameter around a cup on the practice green. Don't worry about making putts; just try to get inside the circle. Having a large target takes the pressure off trying to make the putt and helps you think of just getting the ball within easy tap-in range.

A good drill for those crucial short putts is to put tees in the ground one foot from the cup, two feet, three feet, and so on. Then make five consecutive putts from the first tee, then from the second, and on back to five feet. If you miss a putt, start all over again.

A variation on this drill is putting around the cup in a circle. Putt three-footers around the cup and don't quit until you make every one. Realign and concentrate on each putt. These drills will develop consistency under pressure.

A word of caution about putting practice: It can be hard on your back. I always straighten up between every putt and pause briefly. It's too much stress on your back to stay crouched over in your putting stance for too long.

Two-Handed Putting Drill

The reason most golfers use the reverse-overlapping grip in putting is to make the hands feel as one. The hands feel unified, together, and the risk is reduced of one hand taking over and jerking, pushing or pulling the ball.

Sometimes, though, going to an opposite extreme can help pull you out of a putting slump. Separate your hands in the putting stroke, putting the right hand three or four inches below the left hand. Now try stroking a dozen putts. This will temporarily give you the feeling back. When you go back to your normal stroke, you should have improved your overall feel to the stroke.

Another drill we use in golf schools is to have players experiment with a cross-handed putting grip. The right-handed golfer places his right hand on the top of the grip first and then the left hand below. This will keep the wrists from breaking down on the stroke and prevent the blade from

119

passing through first. This is why many top pros who begin to wrestle with the "yips" turn to a cross-handed stroke. Beginners do well with this as it allows them to feel a pendulum motion in the shoulders and arms.

In Love With Putting

I have yet to see a good putter who didn't think he or she was a good putter, and who didn't love to putt. When I was putting well when I played the tour, sometimes I'd walk up to a green before an attempt at a birdie and think about how much I loved to putt, how I couldn't wait to get up there and strike that putt and watch it go in the hole.

If you're not putting well, fake it until you make it. Think of each putt as an opportunity to make a great birdie or a scrambling par. Hear in your mind that wonderful rattle of the ball falling into the cup. Imagine how much fun it's going to be to pick that ball out of the cup.

If you think like you're going to make it, soon they'll start to fall.

Practice Takes Precision

Ninety-five percent of golfers have no idea how to practice correctly. They bang balls and bang and bang. And they hit the driver until they're worn out. Sometimes I'll ask someone, "What's your target?"

They point to nothing in particular and say, "Out there."

And I respond, "Where, out there?"

Here are some ideas for practice. I guarantee they'll make you a better golfer.

1) I like to put clubs down to mark target alignment and feet alignment, much like railroad tracks. At the very least, put a club down to set your feet in a path parallel to the line of flight. You can also lay a club perpendicular to your track to check your ball position.

2) Play a round of golf on the practice tee. Often if I don't have time to play eighteen holes, I'll tee a ball up on the range, imagine the first hole at Pine Needles, and hit the driver. I'll imagine where it landed, then hit the next shot, a fairway wood on the par-five hole. Then I'll hit a wedge to a target I'll pick out on the range. And so on through the course. You can go so far as to take your putter out and make a couple of strokes.

3) Slow down. There's no prize for hitting the most balls. You'll get better results hitting a small bucket in forty-five minutes than a large bucket in an hour. Go through your pre-shot routine on every shot. Take several practice swings between shots. We have all kind of drills at our schools that we recommend to golfer in order to build a golf swing. You can build a great swing and never hit a ball.

4) Continue to check your grip and grip pressure. You'll tend to grip the club tighter the more balls you hit.

5) And always, have a target for every shot — even on your practice swings.

Babe On The Range

Now I'm going to tell you a story that contradicts everything I just said. Practice is a little different for a beginner. When you're starting from square one, picking targets and playing the course on the practice range won't help much.

Beginners have got to be willing to put some time into their golf games. When Babe Zaharias decided to play golf seriously, she played very little golf for two years and hit a thousand balls and took a thousand practice swings a day. Imagine that!

I'm not saying you have to devote that kind of time to your development. But golf's like anything else in life — what you put in, you'll get out.

I recommend you give your short game more time than your full shots. Vijay Singh says for every hour he spends on his full swing, he spends at least an equal amount of time on his short game.

Distance Versus Direction

Most high-handicappers have their priorities all mixed up on the golf course.

They're obsessed with distance off the tee and how far each of their iron shots travel.

And they'll mimic the tour pros on the putting green, laboring over the break of a putt.

In truth, the priorities work the opposite way:

The short game is distance and the long game is direction.

Think about it.

Most of the time you get into trouble off the tee because of bad direction.

Most of the time when you hit a bad pitch shot from forty yards, it's poor distance.

And most of the time you three-putt, it's because your first putt is way past or way short of the hole.

So when you practice, develop accuracy with the full swing and distance control with the short game.

The Seven-To-Five Drill

Here is a wonderful drill — a must for all beginners and one I use frequently myself.

You simply make small swings, no wrist cock, from seven-to-five on the face of a clock, making sure you extend both arms down the target line through impact. Do this over and over, with a slow, smooth rhythm. Then advance to eight-to-four swings, (little wrist cock), then nine-to-three swings (more wrist cock), on up to your full swing.

Beat The Bag

Another of my favorite training aids is the "Impact Bag." It's a yellow vinyl bag about the size of a large beach ball stuffed with old towels or blankets. You set it on the ground, address it with a golf club, take your swing and hit into the bag.

It's an outstanding device for helping people learn to get out of their banana-ball miseries. Most people who hit the ball from left-to-right — and that's the majority of weekend golfers — don't get the clubface square at impact. I have them think of hitting the bag with the toe of the club at impact. That makes them work on getting the back of the left hand leading through the ball and getting the clubface back to square or slightly closed.

They swing at the impact bag a half dozen times, then hit a few half shots with the ball teed up. Then back to the impact bag, then back to balls. After a while, the light goes on and they're grinning from ear to ear watching the ball fly straight — or maybe even bend from right-to-left. At long last — now they're free to see more of the golf course than the right-hand rough.

Golf's Biggest Fan

Another training aid we love at Pine Needles is the "Power Swing Fan." This is a mock golf club with four fins mounted on the end. You grip it and swing it like a real golf club, and the fins provide resistance to the air. The fan is great for building up strength and power in the golf swing, particularly the all-important left side. The late Bill Strausbaugh, one of the game's truly great teachers and a fixture over the years at Pine Needles at teaching seminars, used to get up before golf instructors and tell them, "This swing fan is a must." Someone asked him how much he was being paid to endorse it, and he said, "Not a penny."

The Dime Drill

Some people pay a hundred dollars for an hour of an instructor's time when a simple dime will give them more solid and consistent golf shots.

The right and left hands need to stay together throughout the swing, but often at the top of the swing, the base of the right hand for a right-handed golfer (below the thumb) will stray somewhat and become disengaged from the left hand. When that happens, you don't get a good cocking or setting of the back of the right hand at the top.

As you address the club in practice, try placing a dime on the base of the left thumb. Now place your right hand over the left in the proper grip. Hit the ball with the dime lodged between the two hands, and keep the hands together so that the dime doesn't drop during the swing. You'll hit the ball flush in no time.

Tip The Tee

Here's another idea for golfers dogged by the banana-ball. This will help you learn to extend your arms through the ball at impact, out toward the target, and get rid of that sidespin that creates the slice.

Get a mid-iron and a handful of tees. Tee the ball up and place a high tee in the ground about six inches in front of the ball. Take half swings and try to hit the ball and then the second tee. In no time you'll be extending through the ball properly and you can graduate to a full swing.

Woods Over Irons

I noticed at the U.S. Women's Open at Pine Needles in 1996 that some of the girls had no long-irons in their bags. They'd stop at the six-iron and after that had lofted fairway woods in their bags — some had as many as six woods. I remember Raymond Floyd winning the U.S. Open in 1986 and using a five-wood instead of longer irons.

The weekend player can certainly learn from that. Lee Trevino once joked that during a thunderstorm he'd walk down the fairway holding a one-iron over his head, "Because even God can't hit a one-iron," he said. The fact is, most ladies and high-handicappers have a hard time hitting a four-iron.

The equipment manufacturers are helping the average player today by making all these lofted woods. They have more mass that helps get the ball airborne, and they're easier to hit with a sweeping blow than the descending blow required for a good, crisp iron shot.

Working The Golf Ball

There are a lot of theories about "working" the golf ball, or creating a curve from left-to-right (a fade to a slice, depending on the degree), or from right-to-left (a draw to a hook, also depending on the degree). Some teachers advocate adjusting the grip. Advanced players can time their release through the ball-delaying the hand action for a fade or ratcheting it up for a draw.

The simplest method for most golfers is this:

To hit a draw or a hook, align your body and feet in the direction you want the ball to start. Then hood the clubface (regrip the club with a closed face) in the direction of your ultimate target.

For a fade or slice, same theory, opposite direction. Line yourself up on the line the ball should start, then open your clubface (regrip the club with an open face) on a line with the eventual target.

Say you have a dogleg right hole with woods along the right side and you've pushed your tee shot into the right rough. You have a good lie and can still make a full swing, but you need to fade the ball around the corner of the dogleg. Stand behind the ball and pick out a line where the ball needs to start. Align your feet and body in that direction. Now open the clubface slightly, so that it's pointing at the green or where you want the second shot to land.

Now take your normal swing. You'll find the ball will start straight down the line, then bend on command around the trees.

126

With a little practice on the range, you can get a good feel for how much a slight adjustment in club-face alignment will mean in ball flight.

Mickey's "Swing-Wright"

Mickey Wright was the finest striker of the ball in women's golf. She was the first big-hitter to come along after Babe Zaharias died in 1956. Galleries wanted to see the ball go back in those days just as they flock to players like Tiger Woods, John Daly and Laura Davies today.

Among the wonderful elements of Mickey's swing back in the sixties and seventies was the connection of her elbows. They were close to her body at address and worked wonderfully together on the backswing, impact and follow through.

In fact, Mickey was the first player I knew of to produce and sell the arm-and-elbow harness that's a popular training aid today and is made by several manufacturers. It was called the "Swing-Wright," and was made by Wilson Sporting Goods. It was a simple elastic strap with a hole for both arms to fit just above the elbows that keeps the arms and elbows "connected" throughout the swing. Look at Ben Hogan. His elbows were really close at address and stayed that way throughout his swing.

The LPGA held the Titleholders at Pine Needles in 1972, and every day Mickey came into my teaching shed at the side of the practice range and put her strap on and hit balls. Later, I learned that strap concept goes back as far as the mid-twenties.

Walter Hagen promoted a device called the "Strok-rite" as far back as 1927.

It remains today one of the best training aids I know. I keep one in my golf bag at all times. Whenever I start hitting the ball inconsistently, I'll strap that thing on, hit a couple dozen balls and soon the ball's flying right. Or Wright, I should say.

The Head Cover Drill

Another great drill for maintaining a proper relationship of the right arm to the body during the swing involves a head cover. Take your address over the ball and slip a head cover under your right armpit. Don't squeeze the head cover between your arm, armpit and upper body, but have just enough pressure to hold the head cover in place throughout impact. By doing that, you'll keep the connection between the right elbow, upper arm and body. I personally prefer the technique of keeping the elbows together so that the right elbow points down throughout the swing. Be careful and don't overdo this drill. It can flatten your swing path.

At the U.S. Open at Pinehurst in 1999, I watched Vijay Singh hit balls for a solid hour with a head cover under his right armpit. He had a great week, finishing tied for third, and went on the following spring to win the Masters. So that tells you something about the value of the head cover drill.

I also saw Vijay tossing a twelve-pound medicine ball to his caddie like he was hitting a golf shot both right and left handed. Just think of the condition he is in to be able to do this.

The Perfect Lie

When I used to take lessons from Tommy Armour at Boca Raton in the 1940s and '50s, he had an assistant tee up every ball, no matter what club I was hitting — wood, long-iron or short-iron. "If you're learning the swing or working on something new, why not give yourself a perfect lie?" Tommy always said.

I've followed that thinking throughout my career, and it still makes good sense. If you're working on something on the practice tee, give yourself a break and make the lie perfect.

The opposite of this drill is a productive one as well. Instead of perfect lies on tees, hit balls out of divots or terrible lies. This teaches you to hit down and through. Hit the ball first, then the turf.

Left Is The Boss

A couple of years ago, I was giving a lesson to my granddaughter, Melody Miller. I was trying to impress upon her the importance of having a strong left side (for a right-handed golfer) in the golf swing, and I told her, "Left is the boss."

She went home and her mother, Peggy Ann asked her, "What did you learn today?"

Melody said, "The left is the boss."

That has stuck in her mind. It's a good thought for you, as well. If the right side overtakes the left, you can hit all kinds of bad shots.

Today Melody is ten years old and has a wonderful golf swing. She'll always remember that "the left is the boss."

The Babe's Secret

Once I asked Babe Zaharias, "Tell me, how do you hit it so far?"

She stretched her right arm around her left shoulder, put her fingers on the part of her back behind the shoulder blade, and said, "I just take it away with that muscle on the backswing, then hit it."

Easier said than done, of course.

But what that underlines is how important the big muscles in the body are to the golf swing. I often use the expression "stretch, and spring," meaning stretch the back on the backswing, then it will spring back through on the downswing. You cannot make a good swing and hit the ball with any power if you don't make a good, full turn back — with your back facing the target.

The Mental Game

All the top professional golfers today have a sports psychologist. We didn't have those in the early days of the LPGA Tour, but I assure you we knew the basic principles that these people taught — we just didn't know we were delving into sports psychology. Today friends like Bob Rotella and Dick Coop have made a specialty out of golf psychology, and they do a great job.

Babe Zaharias wasn't big on hitting balls after playing a tournament round. I'd want to hit balls and she'd say, "I don't need to practice. I can go back to my hotel room, lie down on the bed, replay every shot and get more benefit from that than getting all sweaty beating balls." In those early days, Babe had taken the mental game a notch above everyone else.

Long ago a popular novelty were little flip decks of action sequences — a guy hitting a baseball, swinging a golf club, throwing a football. It would be a little stack of pictures and you'd "flip" them in rapid succession, and you'd see a "real-time" depiction of whatever the motion was.

I had one of those of Sam Snead's golf swing. To me, Sam Snead was the hottest thing going in golf. I loved that fluid motion of his. I carried that little flip deck around with me everywhere and had the rhythm and motion of his swing committed to memory. So anytime I would practice or be on the golf course, I'd visualize Sam's swing. Often I'll recommend that a student close his eyes and swing, allowing him to feel the rhythm and motion of the swing.

I suggest the same thing for any aspiring amateur golfer or even weekend player. When you go to a tournament, find a player whose body size and style fit you. Watch them hit balls and play the golf course. Then try to mimic his tempo and action. You'll be surprised how much that can help.

Remember your good shots and everything about them — the feel of impact, of the club clipping the turf and taking a divot, of watching the ball bore against that blue sky, of your playing partners saying, "Good ball." Then stand over the next shot, expecting everything to happen just as it did before.

Leonard Schmutte, the pro at Findlay Country Club and my first golf teacher, taught me to visualize every shot, to see the ball flying to the target. And this was years before the mental gurus.

One more thing about targets. Pick out a very specific one for every shot, and think of the ball landing on that target as you're getting set to hit. That's called confidence, and nothing breeds successful shots more than a confident mind. You need a mind's eye as well as an optical eye.

Attitude is Everything

Once in the Titleholders, I made a triple bogey on the first hole, a seven, after playing ping-pong in the bunkers around the green. There's nothing worse than starting your round off so horribly. I was playing with Babe Zaharias, and walking to the next tee, she said, "Peggy, see if you can play even par from here."

Babe's words helped me turn loose mentally of the terrible start and accept that what was done, was done. I couldn't have that hole over again.

So I blocked it out mentally and went back to work. I thought to myself there wasn't anything I did wrong on the first hole that I can't correct. And I had a little bad luck as well.

I wound up shooting seventy-four, playing one-under the rest of the day. I was so grateful afterward to Babe and what she'd said to me.

That's where golf is a microcosm for life. You can have a bad day or bad month or bad year. You can sit and stew about it and make things worse, or you can let them go and get on with your life.

Sometimes I'll see people get mad after a bad shot, and I'll tell them, "No one can hit every one perfectly." Look at baseball players. If you're successful thirty percent in batting, you hit for a three hundred average and get rich.

Once I got mad after a bad shot and slammed my club hard to the ground. Babe said, "Do you think you're good enough to hit every one perfect?" I felt terrible and it was the last time I ever did that.

Pat McGowan, my son-in-law and our director of instruction at Pine Needles, puts a sign up when we do a beginners school.

Golf is fun;
Golf is recreation;
Being relaxed and confident allow me to have
a balanced and rhythmical swing.

Set Some Goals

Golf is like anything else in life: You'll achieve more if you set goals and work toward them. When I first started playing golf as a teenager, I was enthralled by the Curtis Cup competition. I decided then and there that I wanted to play in one. From that point, every practice ball I hit, every round I played, every lesson I took, was geared toward helping me achieve that goal. Fortunately, I made the 1950 team.

You can do the same thing. Set a goal to shave five or ten strokes off your handicap; to break eighty at your home course; to qualify for the championship flight. You'll become a better player by defining what you want to accomplish. Every year, many of the ladies who return to my Golfaris are so excited when they have improved their handicap enough that they can go into a more advanced group. I have some ladies who have come as beginners and are now in the advanced group.

My Most Memorable Lesson

The most memorable golf lesson I ever took came in 1949 in Hollywood, Florida. I was hitting the ball horribly and because of that, was going to skip the Titleholders tournament in Augusta. My father had a house near Orange Brook Country Club, where Babe Zaharias and I had teamed to win the International Four-Ball in 1947, so I was always there working on my game.

That day I ran into Al Watrous, the pro from Oakland Hills Country Club in Birmingham, Michigan, who spent winters in Hollywood. "How's it going, Peggy?" he asked.

"Terribly," I cried. "I can't hit the ball. I'm staying home this week."

"Well, let's have a look," Al said.

Everyone who took golf lessons from Al knew he had a unique teaching method. I didn't know about it at the time, but I soon learned.

He watched you hit a few balls, you talked about your problems, then Al grabbed a six-iron and took over.

He hit ball after ball after ball. Between shots, he talked about the feel of the swing, the feel of impact, the follow through, the flight of the ball. It was the craziest lesson I'd ever taken. I wanted to hit the balls. I thought — Boy, he must keep his game in shape!

At the time I'd begun cupping my left wrist on the backswing and thus had an open clubface at the top and was hitting everything to the right. Al talked about "grabbing back" with the last three fingers of the left hand at the top, so that my wrist would be flat at the top instead of cupping.

I only hit about ten balls, but he left me a mental image and some swing cues after he hit balls for about an hour. He'd stop and ask, "What do you see?" I had a picture and a feel for what I was trying to do. He would ask, "Do you see the pattern for the swing?" "Can you repeat what you see?" Years later, touring pro Al Geiberger made a tape for visualization of the golf swing that helped so many golfers.

I started hitting it like dynamite, and all of a sudden my confidence was back. I went home and packed, jumped on a plane and flew to Augusta. Without a practice round, I won the Titleholders, breaking the tournament record!

Al's method worked wonderfully for me at that time and it gave me the feel of the golf swing. He was so well known over decades as a teacher and player that today there's a street named after him at the PGA Headquarters in Palm Beach Gardens, Florida.

Ladies' Tour: A Men's Clinic

Every weekend golfer — men in particular — can get a valuable lesson from the practice tee at an LPGA event. In fact, I run across men all the time who tell me what a great time they have at women's tour events. The reason is that average players can relate to the women's game much better than to the men's professional tours.

The men pros have games and swings with which few mortals can identify. They swing so hard, albeit very much in control and on rhythm. The ball goes so far. Their shots are marvelous, for sure, but it's hard to relate to them.

People can relate better to the women's swing. Their tempo is smoother. Their swings are a little slower and you can see what's going on. Men tell me they watch those girls' fluid swings for half an hour and then, next time they play, they try to emulate the pros and they get much crisper golf shots. Men can also take a cue from women and their fondness for five- and seven-woods. They're a lot easier to get airborne than long irons.

Golf: A Walking Game

Golf was meant to be played on foot, and it does me good to see people out walking the golf course. Of course, when you get to be my age, a cart makes playing golf possible, so I shouldn't knock them.

If you're healthy enough and young enough to walk, do it!

Can you imagine Donald Ross in a golf cart? I cannot.

I think golf carts are one of the culprits of slow play. When you have two people in a cart, you drive to one ball, and that player gets ready to hit and then hits his shot. It's usually not until he finishes, puts his club back in his bag, and they drive on to the next golfer's ball that the second player starts to examine his shot, the yardage, the wind, etc. If you're carrying your bag or playing with a caddie, you go directly to your ball and prepare for your shot while everyone else is doing the same. It makes for ready golf!

Our family's resorts in Southern Pines, Pine Needles and Mid Pines, are two of the few golf resorts in the country that will allow you a choice — walk or ride, any time, any day, same price. We've also developed a caddie program, using students in the Professional Golf Management program at Methodist College in Fayetteville.

How better to enjoy the conversation of your playing partners while walking from tee to fairway, from approach shot to green, from green to the next hole? Or, if you prefer, enjoy complete solitude? Ever notice when riding that the players in the other cart might as well be in another foursome for all the conversation you have during the round?

If you walk, your game is not confounded with the constant stopping and starting of golf carts. You can watch the birds, smell the roses, feel the quirky undulations of the ground under your feet, and kick back after your round with that feeling you've gotten some exercise.

We had the first golf carts in the Sandhills area at Pine Needles in 1953. Since Peggy Kirk Bell clubs were sold through Sears, I was able to buy a golf cart there for about $600. It had three wheels, a rounded front and a steering stick. I thought it might be a nice novelty to have around the resort, maybe a quick way to get from one lodge to another, but I never dreamed carts would become second nature to so many golfers. Richard Tufts, the owner of Pinehurst, said there'd never be a golf cart on

Pinehurst property. Little did he know what would happen in the game.

We do our best at Pine Needles and Mid Pines to make caddies available during prime season. They're an important institution in golf, and you've never really played the game unless you've played an old Donald Ross course with a caddie by your side.

Kids Golf: Grip And Fun

There are only two things about teaching children to play golf that are important. One, get their grip right from the beginning. Two, let them have fun.

There are exceptions, of course, but generally speaking, you can't play good golf unless you have a good grip. And changing a bad one after years of getting accustomed to it is very, very difficult. So if you're going to introduce golf to a child, get the grip right from the beginning. (Some children are too young to use a traditional grip from the beginning and do better with a ten-finger grip. That's fine, but just make sure their hands are facing each other — as they would if they were praying — when they grip the club. Then when their hands are big enough, they can move to a standard grip.)

Beyond that, just let them have fun. Give them attainable goals — like letting them tee off on every hole from the 150-yard markers. It's fine to teach them the fundamentals — such as posture and swing path — but don't get hung up on beating balls and learning swing techniques. Kids will make a natural swing at the ball that will surprise you. They're great mimics. Show them a swing and say, "Copy that." Give them a good grip and let them fall in love with golf on their own. Then you've got a lifetime to teach them technique.

And If You Can't Learn Golf ....

I think all professionals and teachers are always learning. One day during a break at a Golfari I was trying to peel a banana. I was trying to break it at the end with the stalk, and the stalk wouldn't tear. I knew I was squishing the inside of the banana and it would be a mess if I ever got the stupid thing open.

A lady came up to me and said, "Would you like to know how to peel a banana?"

I welcomed her advice. She turned the banana around and peeled it from the bottom. Sure enough, the skin pulled away easily in neat little strips.

"That's the way a monkey peels a banana," she said.

Always go to the expert, I say, and I guess a monkey's an expert on a banana.

At the end of the week, I stood up and told the group, "If you haven't learned anything about the golf swing this week, never fear. You're going to leave with one important lesson." I had the gal come up and demonstrate the art of peeling the banana.

So don't say you never learned anything from Peggy Kirk Bell.

Peggy Kirk Bell's
Tournament Championships

- 1947, 1948, 1949 Ohio Women's Amateur
- 1949 Women's North and South Amateur
- 1947 International Four-Ball (with Babe Zaharias)
- 1949 Titleholders Championship
- 1950 Eastern Amateur
- 1950 Curtis Cup Team
- 1948 Curtis Cup Team Alternate
- 1951 LPGA Weathervane Team
- Florida Mixed Two-Ball (with Joe Kirkwood)
- Everglades Two-Ball
- Palm Beach Amateur

Peggy Kirk Bell's
Honors and Awards

- Inducted into the LPGA
  (Teaching Division), HALL OF FAME 2000
- Top LPGA Master Professional, 1985
- Top 50 Teachers — Golf for Women, 1990-2000
- N.C. High School Athletic Association
  Legend Award, 1999
- Member — Jack Nicklaus Captain's Club
  The Memorial Tournament, Inducted, 1998
- North Carolina Governor's Award, 1998
- Distinguished Women of N.C. Award, 1992
- Golf Digest's top five most influential women in Golf
- Former Board Member and now Life Trustee
  Fellowship of Christian Athletes
- Fellowship of Christian Athletes Hall of Fame
- Honorary Chairman,
  U.S. Women's Open Golf Championship, 1996 - 2001
- Golf Writers Assn. Of America's
  William Richardson Award, 1993
- USGA Bob Jones Award, 1990
- LPGA Teacher of the Year, 1961

North Carolina Sports Hall of Fame, 1976
- Carolina's Golf Hall of Fame, 1981
- Ohio Golf Hall of Fame, 1981
- Toledo Golf Hall of Fame, 2000
- Inaugural LPGA Rolex Ellen Griffin Award, 1989
- Received Honorary Doctorate at University of Findlay
- Received Honorary Doctorate at Methodist College
- Received Honorary Doctorate at
  Sandhills Community College

Tournament Championships

- Palm Beach Breakers Amateur
- Florida Mixed Two-Ball — 3 times (with Joe Kirkwood)
- Western Open 1950 (runner-up to Helen Wilson)
- Western Amateur 1949 (runner-up to Helen Wilson)